CONTENTS

S0-BRM-408

Introduction

After thousands of years as a dietary staple, rice, which provides the chief source of food for six out of every ten humans, has finally become fashionable in America. Health-conscious Americans are eating more rice than ever before—twenty-two pounds of rice per person last year.

With rice's growing popularity in this country, electric rice cookers have been "discovered" too. The rice cooker is simple to use: once the rice and water are added to the cooker to steam, it can be forgotten. Set your cooker up as a separate station in a corner of the kitchen to free your stove top and your attention for other cooking tasks.

For centuries Asians have understood the advantages of steaming foods, while other cultures have relied far less on this cooking method. Foods cooked with steam retain their natural flavors and have a fluffy texture that the Italians refer to as *vaporoso*. This sensible and efficient method preserves valuable nutrients from being washed away.

Steaming has been made simpler with the proliferation of multipurpose electric rice cookers, as well as heavy-duty cookware containing steaming baskets. The cook can easily adapt most recipes to work in whatever equipment is used.

Easy-to-follow recipes in this cookbook focus on America's infatuation with the foods of the Mediterranean and other exotic locales such as Thailand, India, and China, where meals routinely center on rice. Rice is either served with main dishes or is the major ingredient in most recipes. You will also find numerous recipes for using leftover rice, as well as for time-honored rice favorites in this country, like hoppin' John and rice pudding.

Cooking with Steam

Steaming is easy and, best of all, natural flavors are retained in the process, so steamed foods taste delicious. Steaming preserves valuable nutrients. Many vitamins and minerals are water-soluble, so if the cooking liquid is not consumed, they are lost. The primary advantage of steaming is that foods can be cooked without adding fat; for every tablespoon of fat you eliminate from your diet, deduct a hundred calories.

Choosing an Electric Rice Cooker

Before you buy an electric rice cooker, investigate different models. There are two basic types on the market today, but individual features differ greatly. Over the past few years, a wide range of electric rice cookers in a variety of styles and materials have appeared. With some knowledge about the basic designs and how they are typically used, you will be able to choose the best one to fit your needs.

Common Rice Cooker

The original electric rice cooker works on the same principle as the boil-and-steam method for steaming rice on top of the stove. Rice and water are combined in a solid pan that fits inside a shell with a heating element in its base (Figure 1). This type does not

Figure 1

have a water reservoir. The pan is covered, the cooker is switched on, and when the element detects the complete absorption of water, the machine shuts off automatically. The rice continues to steam until the grains are tender.

Use of your rice cooker need not be limited to rice and rice dishes. Beyond perfect rice every time, the rice cooker can steam, braise, sauté, or stir-fry a wide variety of foods, or act as a food warmer (depending on the model).

Steaming pans, steaming baskets, and/or racks are included with most appliances, or can be ordered for most sizes. A flat metal plate with tiny perforations that fits flush against the bottom of the pan is used in some models. Special pans with lids can also be ordered. Or lids can be fashioned out of tinfoil, to prevent excess moisture from getting into the food.

Some models have a "warm" setting that holds rice at the proper temperature without drying it out. Hitachi's Chime-O-Matic model rings to let you know the rice has absorbed the water and is now steaming, so you can plan the rest of the meal accordingly. Nonstick inner pans, clear lids, or high and low temperature settings are available on certain models.

Rice cookers are available in a variety of sizes. A large (ten-cup) model is best for a family of four. Enormous commercial rice cookers can be purchased in Asian supermarkets or variety stores in major cities. The original rice cooker market is dominated by Japanese manufacturers.

Above-the-Water Type

Americans have discovered the advantages of cooking with steam, and the number of multipurpose, above-the-water type electric rice cookers and steamers has increased to support the demand. The features on each model vary considerably.

The above-the-water rice cooker has a reservoir with a heating element in the bottom. The reservoir is filled with water and the element heats the water to produce steam. The steam circulates around the food container above the reservoir.

Some models come with two containers, one with holes for steaming vegetables (a steamer basket) and the other (a pan) for cooking rice with liquid as well as foods with a sauce. Usually the containers cannot be used at the same time.

There is no on/off switch on some models; the appliance is turned on and off with the plug. When the water has evaporated, the timer light goes out, but the steamer does not turn itself off. The cook must remember to remove the plug.

Sizes and shapes vary from the traditional round shape (Figure 2) to Rival's distinctive oval-shaped model (Figure 3), which can accommodate sweet corn or a whole fish.

More sophisticated cookers come with high and low temperature settings. Other desirable features include an on/off switch, a timer, and a buzzer. The Excalibur Steam Cuisine II has

Figure 2

Figure 3

all of these features, and is capable of cooking three foods at the same time.

Most manufacturers of small appliances in the United States now include at least one above-the-water electric rice cooker/steamer in their line. Rival, Waring, Salton, Black & Decker, and Betty Crocker are well-known names.

Timing Your Electric Rice Cooker

Experiment with your equipment to learn its individual features so you can cook food the way you like it. Follow the manufacturer's directions precisely at first. If the food isn't cooked enough for your taste, increase the amount of liquid. If it is over-cooked, decrease the amount of liquid used.

Cooking time will depend on the type of rice cooker you use and the amount and size of the food being cooked. For example, sliced potatoes will be ready before whole ones. Steaming time is generally the same, or slightly longer, than oven-cooking time. It takes a little practice with your particular cooker to determine accurate cooking times.

Don't overload your cooker. Produce cooks more evenly if placed in a single layer. If foods are packed tightly, cooking takes longer, because steam cannot circulate freely.

Steaming time will vary according to whether items are placed in a steaming basket or directly on the rack. Foods cooked in a steaming pan on the rack of a steamer take a little longer. Remember, the closer the rack is to water, the faster the food will cook. Foods also cook faster if they start out at room temperature when steamed. If ingredients come straight from the refrigerator, time may need to be increased.

Take into consideration that foods continue to cook in a covered pot once the heat is turned off. Be especially alert when steaming vegetables or fish since they can easily overcook.

Adapting Favorite Recipes

Read the manufacturer's instructions that come with your electric rice cooker and follow them exactly; they will vary depending on the type of model you chose. Once you understand the workings of your individual appliance, you will be able to adapt most recipes by simply decreasing or increasing the amount of liquid. (Rice cookers usually require one-fourth to one-half cup less liquid than conventional cooking methods.)

Read the entire recipe first, then decide which steps can be done in your appliance. For example, if the recipe calls for sautéing onion or garlic in oil first, this step can be done in most boil-and-steam type rice cookers, but not in the above-the-water types. Sauté in a separate pan, or simply steam the vegetables in a little broth or water.

Some adaptations do not work. The success of certain recipes depends on other cooking techniques. But many favorites do fare well when steamed. The recipes in this book are dishes you can cook with your new rice cooker depending on its size and capabilities.

Timing begins when the unit is plugged in. When adapting recipes, adjust timing to include a warm-up period with the steaming times given.

A special measuring cup that contains less than a standard measuring cup is supplied with some rice cookers. For recipes in this book, a standard measuring cup was used.

White (Carolina) rice was used to test the recipes in this book, but feel free to substitute and experiment with the great varieties of rice now available.

General Tips

These tips highlight situations you may face when you use your electric rice cooker for the first few times. Suggestions for your specific appliance should be found in the manual that came with it. Read and follow the manufacturer's instructions carefully. Each type of cooker has its own peculiarities.

- Steaming times will vary depending on desired doneness, food quantity, size, and arrangement. Altitude, humidity, and outside temperatures also affect cooking times.
- To adjust steaming time, add or delete amount of steaming liquid.
- Always keep lid on the cooker during entire steaming process unless instructed otherwise. Opening the lid causes a loss of heat and steam and will slow the cooking time. If you must remove the lid, have everything ready to stir and/or add.
- To check food during and just after steaming, lift the cover away from you, letting water drip down into the reservoir, not into the dish. Let water drip onto a towel or a dish when using a boil-and-steam type cooker.
- To avoid steam burns, use long-handled utensils/tongs and pot holders.
- If burned by steam, immediately put the burned area under cold running water and leave it there until the pain ceases.
- If your rice is sticking, add a light coating of vegetable oil to the inner pot before adding rice and water.
- Do not place the electric rice cooker/steamer too close to wooden or laminated cabinet doors when operating. It produces large amounts of steam which may cause warping.
- A thin white film on the interior reservoir of above-the-water type cookers may develop due to minerals in the water. Wash after each use with distilled white vinegar.
- Some foods that are steamed need to be covered to prevent excess moisture from getting into the foods. Foods

such as custard that need a cover are specified in the manufacturer's steaming guide. Tinfoil can be used to make a lid.

- Always unplug your rice cooker and allow to cool before cleaning.

Additional Steaming Equipment

The Chinese use two pairs of chopsticks in a tic-tac-toe pattern as a platform in the bottom of a wok when they want to steam a dish. A canning jar ring, a trivet, or even an empty tuna-fish can with both ends removed can be used as platforms to turn a variety of pots into steamers. Electric frying pans with high dome lids can be adapted easily.

To help you round out your collection of steaming equipment, here is a list of specialized steaming devices commonly used today.

- *Stainless steel collapsible basket*   This inexpensive rack with expanding panels has become a kitchen classic (Figure 4). It fits into a wide range of pot sizes and is especially suited for steaming vegetables.
- *Chinese bamboo steamer*   These steamers come in many sizes, have no base, and are made to be set onto a wok containing boiling water (Figure 5). They are convenient

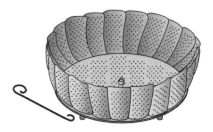

Figure 4

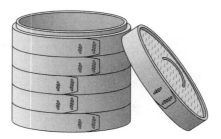

Figure 5

in that they come in layers, so that several dishes can be steamed at once.

- *Tiered steamer* An all-purpose steamer with one or two tiers (Figure 6). The food that takes longest to cook goes in the lower tier, the fastest-cooking on top. If both foods require the same cooking time, tiers are switched halfway through. Tiered steamers come in a wide range of materials, most frequently aluminum or enamelware.
- *Yunnan pot* This unique ceramic pot, which looks like an angel food cake pan with a lid (Figure 7), originated in the southwestern province of China. The pot sits over a pan of boiling water. As water boils, steam rises through the chimney and lightly mists the food before

Figure 6

Figure 7

condensing. Chinatown stores carry Yunnan pots in one-, two-, and three-quart sizes, and one-of-a-kind pots can often be found at craft fairs.

- *Dish retrieving tool*   This three-pronged tool automatically adjusts to the size of a dish thus solving the problem of how to grapple a hot dish out of boiling water without spilling it or burning yourself. Available with canning supplies and in Chinese or other Asian stores.

Cooking with Rice

America's interest in rice is a fairly recent phenomenon, and rice now rivals pasta as the basis for all kinds of main dishes. Many ethnic cuisines center around rice or other carbohydrates, and over the past decade or two Americans have discovered that these dishes can be satisfying without being fattening, if appropriately sauced.

Rice is probably our most versatile food. Bland in flavor and nonallergenic, it combines equally well with poultry, meat, seafood, vegetables, and dairy products to make some of the world's most memorable dishes: *paella* from Spain, *calas* from New Orleans, *picadilla* from Mexico, *risottos* from Italy, Chinese *fried rice*, and Greek *Avgolemono*.

There is no waste in rice. Every particle is edible. What's more, there is no peeling or scraping. It comes ready to cook. Rice, because of its built-in convenience, is easily turned into dinner.

What Is Rice?

Rice is an annual cereal grass that originated in India and China. It was introduced into the West first by way of Egypt and then Greece, where it was already prized at the time of the philosopher Theophrastus (c. 372–287 B.C.). Its popularity spread to Portugal, then to Italy and to America.

Its wild ancestor has been identified as *Oryza sativa*, a semi-aquatic marsh grass native to India and southeast Asia. Most cultivated rice, known as *aquatic rice,* is grown in marshy or flooded lands, the sort of terrain found through much of the southern Orient and southeastern United States.

In the early eighteenth century, rice was widely grown in the Carolinas and Georgia. It can also be grown in areas where there is a long growing season and a great deal of steady rainfall. This type is called *hill rice.* With the mechanization of agriculture, rice-growing moved west to Louisiana. Today American rice is grown primarily in Arkansas, California, Louisiana, Texas, Mississippi, and Missouri. Rice yields more per acre than wheat or corn. Wheat or barley must be ground first, but rice can be eaten as a grain.

Rice is a highly nutritious and easily digested food. Almost all of it is assimilated. When milled so that only the husks are removed, producing *whole* or *brown rice,* 88 percent of it consists of nutrients—about 9 percent protein and 79 percent carbohydrates with very small amounts of fat.

In modern processing, harvested rice goes to a drying plant where hot air is blown through it to "cure" it and reduce its moisture content, assuring good keeping quality. The first step in the milling process is the removal of the husk, leaving what is sometimes called *natural brown rice.* If the milling is carried further, the next step involves the grinding away of several outer layers of the grain. This results in *white rice.* It also produces such by-products as *rice bran* and *rice polishings.*

In the next step all broken particles and any foreign seeds or defective grains are screened out, leaving clean white rice. The finer particles of broken rice can be used in making beer. Years ago, rice was given a coating of talc or glucose, which is why old recipes say "wash rice until the water runs clean."

Nowadays this is not necessary when domestic rice comes in a package. Caution should still be used when using imported rice. Follow directions closely.

Forms of Rice

The three most commonly used forms of rice in this country are white, brown, and parboiled or converted rice.

- *White rice* has the hull and bran layer removed, as well as another coating when polished, but it is not a scourge on humanity as some might have you believe. On the contrary, the discovery that refining rice would allow it to be stored for longer periods without spoiling or becoming pest-infested has kept much of the world from starvation. Modern-day polished rice is also enriched with nutrients lost in processing.
- *Brown rice* is not a separate variety. It is any type of rice from which only the outer hull has been removed during milling, leaving the bran layer behind. It boasts a full, nutty flavor. Rich in vitamins of the B complex—thiamine, niacin, and riboflavin—and in iron and calcium, brown rice is a naturally nutritious product.
- *Parboiled rice* or *converted rice* has been steam-pressure treated before milling, forcing all the nutrients from the bran layer into the grain. Quick to prepare, the grains remain separate and firm-textured when cooked. This method has been used in India for two thousand years.

Varieties of Rice

Educated cooks are no longer cooking with just any old rice, but are using specific varieties of this grain, depending on the desired result. About forty thousand varieties of rice exist; the three main categories—long grain, medium grain, and short grain— vary considerably in taste and texture.

- *Long grain rice* grows best in hot, humid climates and is higher in a starch called *amylose* so the grains cook up separate and fluffy. Most aromatic varieties such as *basmati rice* are included in this broad category.

- *Medium grain rice* is higher in a different starch, *amylopectin,* which makes the grains cook moist and tender, with a slight stickiness. Short, oval-shaped *arborio rice,* the variety used for Italian risottos, is a medium grain rice, as are many rices grown in California. Rices grown in Italy and Spain are medium grain.
- *Short grain rice* is even softer and stickier than medium grain. Both medium and short grain varieties thrive in cooler temperatures. In Japan it is known as *sushi rice.*

Favorite Varieties

American adaptations of long grain basmati rice, as well as the short, oval-shaped arborio rice, are almost as much in demand these days as pasta varieties were a few years ago.

- *Aromatic* is a term used for all sorts of rices that have a subtle, nutty flavor and an aroma something like popcorn. Aromatics include Konriko wild pecan (no nut in sight), Texmati, and jasmine as well as basmati, among others.
- *Basmati* is a long grain rice grown in the Himalaya foothills that gets longer rather than wider as it cooks and has just a hint of nuttiness. The Hindu word *basmati* means "queen of fragrance."
- *Jasmine* is an aromatic long grain rice originally grown only in Thailand but now cultivated in the United States. (A well-known brand is Jasmati.) The grains are similar in size to long grain rice, but cook moist and tender like a medium grain rice. It has a slightly sweet taste.
- *Texmati* is a cross of basmati and an American long grain rice developed in Texas, available in both white and brown rice versions.
- *Wehani* is an aromatic rice that turns an ocher or rust color when cooked. The flavor is evocative of oatmeal and nuts.

- *Arborio* is the variety used for creamy Italian risottos. Like other medium grain rice, it is best cooked until still slightly firm in the center.
- *Valencia* is a medium grain rice grown in the province of Valencia in Spain. A favorite rice in paella, it is available on a limited basis in specialty food shops.
- *Glutinous rice*   Also known as sticky, waxy, or sweet rice, glutinous rice is popular in East Asian cuisines for its soft, sticky texture. Often used in desserts.
- *Rizcous* are tiny chunks of brown rice that look and taste like the semolina product called *couscous*.
- *Wild rice* is not a rice at all, but an aquatic grass with a chewy texture and a nutty flavor, native to the Great Lakes region of the Midwest where it was traditionally harvested by Chippewa Indians. It is now cultivated extensively in California.
- *Rice blends* are innovative combinations of brown and dark rices, many grown and packed by Lundberg Family Farms in Richvale, California.
- *Black japonica* is a medium grain rice with a black bran, grown on a limited basis by the Lundberg family, and used primarily in their mixed rice products.

Nutritional Facts

Rice is not only high in complex carbohydrates—the fuel nutritionists tell us we should be eating more of—but also contains just a trace of fat and sodium. (Check the nutritional information on packaged rice mixes, however, since they can be overloaded with sodium.) Rice is also a fair source of B vitamins and minerals and contains all eight essential amino acids.

A half cup of hot, cooked white rice has 103 calories. The same amount of brown rice has 106 calories.

How Much Rice Should You Cook?

Since rice increases in bulk at least three times when cooked, allow one cup of rice for each three to six servings, depending upon whether it is an accompaniment to meats and vegetables or the basis of a one-dish meal.

1 cup regular white rice	=	3 cups cooked rice
1 cup brown rice	=	4 cups cooked rice
1 cup parboiled or converted rice	=	4 cups cooked rice

How to Store Rice

Store in an airtight container in a cool, dry place. White rice and wild rice will keep indefinitely when stored properly. Brown rice will keep approximately six months after opening, due to the oil in the bran covering. Refrigeration of brown rice will prolong its life.

Cooked rice can be refrigerated for about a week. When refrigerating rice, be sure to cover it with foil or plastic wrap or transfer it to a container with a tight-fitting lid so that the grains will not dry out or absorb the flavors of other foods. Rice should be completely cold when covered or it will become soggy. Rice can be frozen for about three months.

CHAPTER 1

Rice in Soups

*R*ice is an important part of any number of delicious soups. With hearty soups like Lentils and Rice, or Risi e Bisi, little attention is needed until it is time to combine the rice with the soup base and serve.

Although not usually thought of first when preparing soup, your rice cooker can be put to good use because of the popularity of rice in a variety of well-known soups. Unless rice is simmered in broth for a long time until very tender, as in the great Greek soup Avgolemono, rice is best cooked separately so that it retains its firm texture and then added to the finished soup. Allow it to absorb the flavors of the broth for a few minutes before serving.

Leftover steamed vegetables can easily be transformed into soup. Use your imagination to create your own versions. Prepare a simple soup by pureeing a favorite steamed vegetable and heating with seasonings and enough chicken or vegetable stock to form the consistency you desire. Flavor richly with fresh herbs, and if you wish, add cream to create a marvelous soup.

Avgolemono Soup

(*Greek Egg and Lemon Soup*)

One of the truly great, simple soups of the world.

1 quart chicken broth
1 cup cooked rice
2 eggs
Juice of 1 lemon
1 tablespoon minced fresh parsley

Bring broth to boil; add cooked rice. Lower heat; simmer rice until very tender, about 10 minutes. While rice is cooking, beat eggs until light and foamy. Beat in lemon juice. Stir in 1 cup hot soup; blend well. Add egg-and-lemon mixture to rest of soup, stirring constantly. Heat almost to boiling point, but not quite or the soup will curdle. Adjust seasoning if necessary. Serve immediately. Sprinkle with minced fresh parsley.

Serves 4

Variations

• Substitute port wine for lemon juice and call it Portuguese Rice Soup.
• Make an Italian version by beating together 2 egg yolks, juice of 1/2 lemon or to taste, 1/4 cup freshly grated Parmesan cheese, and 2 tablespoons water. Pour mixture into soup, stirring constantly.

Risi e Bisi

This famous Venetian dish is considered by Italians to be a soup, but it is even thicker than most Italian soups.

1 tablespoon butter or olive oil
2 slices prosciutto (Italian ham), minced
1 scallion with green top, minced
1 medium stalk celery with leaves, chopped
2 cups fresh peas, or 1 (10-ounce) package frozen peas, thawed
 and drained
2 cups hot chicken broth
Salt and freshly ground black pepper
3 cups hot cooked rice
1 tablespoon butter
1 tablespoon freshly grated Parmesan cheese

Melt butter; add prosciutto, scallion, and celery. Sauté until vegetables are limp. (This type of sautéed mixture is called *soffrito* or *battuto* in Italian.) Add peas for a moment until well coated. Combine with broth; season with salt and black pepper to taste. Simmer 5 minutes.

Stir in hot rice, butter, and grated cheese. Allow to rest 5 minutes. Serve with additional cheese, if desired.

Serves 4

Variation

- The combination of rice and peas is traditional, but other vegetables such as string beans, mushrooms, or sliced zucchini can be substituted.

Chinese Egg Drop Soup

Egg drop soup is a great Western favorite.

1 quart chicken broth
1/4 cup cornstarch
1 egg, well beaten
Fried or baked rice crust (optional)
1 scallion with green top, chopped

Bring broth to boil; adjust seasoning if necessary. Blend cornstarch with a little hot broth. Stir cornstarch mixture into
chicken broth. Simmer 1 minute or until soup has thickened;
turn off heat. Add beaten egg in a thin stream, stirring constantly
in a circular fashion so that egg forms thin shreds in the hot
broth. Pour over fried or baked rice crust in individual bowls.
Sprinkle with scallions. Serve immediately.

Serves 4

Chinese Rice Crust

Rice crust, or cake, is the firm, crisp mass that forms when ordinary rice is left over low heat for an hour or so after most of the rice has been removed from the pan. The overcooked rice on the bottom takes on a golden color and a nutty flavor. This crust is traditionally deep-fried, but a rice crust can also be made by pressing cooked rice firmly in a shallow baking pan. Bake at 250°F until rice is completely dried out, about 30 minutes. Soup is often poured on the rice crust at the table, making it sizzle or sing dramatically. Try it with Egg Drop Soup.

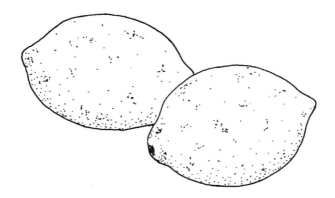

Lentils and Rice Soup

In America, lentils are mostly eaten in soups. Italians consider hearty soup like this their soul food.

1 ½ quarts water
Pinch of salt
1 cup dry lentils (about ½ pound), cleaned and washed
2 tablespoons olive oil
1 clove garlic, halved
1 (8-ounce) can tomato sauce
½ teaspoon salt
¼ teaspoon freshly ground black pepper to taste
½ teaspoon dried basil
1 tablespoon minced fresh parsley
3 cups hot cooked rice
Freshly grated Parmesan cheese

Bring salted water to boil in soup pot. (Lentils dance in water so a smaller pot is better.) Add lentils; simmer for 30 minutes or until lentils are almost tender. Drain, reserving liquid.

Ten minutes before lentils are done, sauté garlic in olive oil in nonstick pan until limp but not brown. Add tomato sauce; simmer 5 minutes. Add 1 cup reserved liquid from lentils if too dry. Add drained lentils, salt, black pepper, basil, and parsley to sauce; simmer gently 5 minutes.

Mix with hot cooked rice; allow to rest 5 minutes before serving. Soup will be very dry. Add more reserved liquid from lentils if you wish. Serve with freshly grated Parmesan cheese.

Serves 4

Variations

- Use canned white cannellini or navy beans instead of lentils. Rinse and drain before adding to tomato sauce.
- Vary flavor of sauce by sautéing with the garlic: 1 small onion and 1 stalk celery with leaves, both finely chopped. Proceed as directed.

Minestrone

Who can resist Italy's most famous soup? Use whatever vegetables are in season.

2 tablespoons olive oil
1 medium onion, chopped
1 clove garlic, minced
1 1/2 quarts water or beef broth
1 medium tomato, cored and chopped, or 2 tablespoons
    tomato sauce
1 stalk celery with leaves, chopped
3 carrots, diced
2 small potatoes, peeled and diced
1 cup string beans, cleaned and cut in 1-inch pieces
2 medium zucchini, diced
1/2 teaspoon salt
1/4 teaspoon freshly ground black pepper
1 tablespoon minced fresh parsley
1 tablespoon minced fresh basil
3 cups hot cooked rice
Freshly grated Parmesan cheese

Sauté onion and garlic in hot oil until limp and golden. Add water, vegetables, salt, pepper, parsley, and basil. Bring to boil; lower heat; simmer 45 minutes. Add cooked rice; simmer 5 minutes. Adjust seasoning if necessary. Serve with Parmesan cheese.

Serves 4 to 6

Variations

• Add rice to individual soup servings if soup is going to be eaten at different times.
• Minestrone recipe can be doubled or tripled.

Chicken Escarole Soup with Rice

Escarole, which is somewhat bitter, adds a nice dimension to ever-popular chicken rice soup.

2 tablespoons olive oil
1 small head escarole (about 1 pound), cleaned, washed,
   and chopped
1 quart chicken broth
2 cups hot cooked rice
Freshly grated Parmesan cheese

Steam or sauté escarole with olive oil for 2 to 3 minutes until wilted. Heat broth; add escarole; simmer 5 minutes. Add hot cooked rice; simmer gently 5 minutes. Serve sprinkled with grated cheese.

Serves 4

Variation

• Sauté garlic clove in olive oil until limp. Discard garlic. Add 2 tablespoons tomato sauce or 2 diced plum tomatoes. Cook until blended. Add escarole and chicken broth. Proceed as directed.

Mulligatawny Soup

There are many versions of this East Indian chicken soup seasoned with curry. Juice of lime is added just before serving.

1 slice bacon, diced, or 2 tablespoons olive oil
1 carrot, diced
3 medium onions, sliced
1 small turnip, chopped
2 tablespoons curry
Pinch of cayenne pepper
1/4 cup flour
Salt to taste
1 tablespoon minced fresh parsley
1 clove garlic, minced
1 stalk rhubarb, chopped
1 quart chicken broth
Juice of 1 lime
3 cups hot cooked rice

If using bacon, fry until crisp. Otherwise, heat olive oil in soup pot. Add carrot, onions, and turnip; sauté 3 minutes, stirring occasionally. Sprinkle with curry, cayenne pepper, and flour; blend well. Cook until onion is limp and golden. Season with salt to taste. Add parsley, garlic, rhubarb, and broth; bring to boil. Lower heat; simmer gently 45 minutes. Just before serving, add lime juice. Adjust seasoning if necessary. Serve with hot rice passed separately.

Serves 4

Split Pea and Rice Soup

The peas and rice in this hearty, savory soup should be al dente—not mushy.

2 tablespoons olive oil
2 medium onions, chopped
2 quarts water
2 cups dried split peas, cleaned and drained
1/2 teaspoon salt
1/4 teaspoon freshly ground black pepper
3 cups hot cooked rice

Sauté onions in hot oil until limp and golden. Combine with water, split peas, salt, and pepper. Simmer soup until peas are tender, about 45 minutes. Adjust seasoning if necessary. Add cooked rice to finished soup; allow to rest 5 minutes before serving.

Serves 4 to 6

Variations

- Instead of olive oil, fry 1 slice of bacon until crisp. Drain off all fat except 1 tablespoon. Sauté onions in bacon fat. Combine with other ingredients as directed.
- Omit olive oil or bacon. Add a ham bone to soup ingredients.

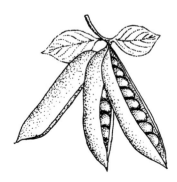

CHAPTER 2

Rice Side Dishes

Cooking rice is a skill that doesn't come easily to many of us. Overcooking, which reduces rice to a mush, has contributed to the disfavor in which rice was held in the West until quite recently. (During the 1870–71 siege of Paris, when there was a shortage of bread, enormous quantities of rice remained unused.)

Rice cookers cook perfect rice every time. Long a favorite appliance in Asian homes, they are found in more and more American homes. Over a million rice cookers are sold every year in the United States.

Since Hitachi introduced its all-purpose Chime-O-Matic Food Steamer/Rice Cooker a decade ago, the common rice cooker has been transformed into a practical unit that need no longer be restricted to cooking just rice. Each cooker has its own features and variations, so whichever one you choose, follow the manufacturer's directions on how to cook rice. Cooking times and quantity of liquid vary considerably.

Preparing gourmet dishes such as pilaf, where each grain is separate and dry, yet tender (not gummy and sticky), requires few steps in your rice cooker. Closer attention is needed to obtain the creamy texture of an Italian risotto, which traditionally requires the addition of liquids in small quantities and frequent stirring throughout the cooking process.

Read recipes carefully. Decide which steps can be done in your rice cooker and which steps should be done in other equipment.

Testing for Tenderness

The easiest way to tell if rice is ready to eat is to taste it. Scoop out a few grains and bite into them. The grains should have no hardness in the center. As soon as grains are tender all through but still firm, the rice is done.

Steamed Rice

Steaming is probably the most popular method used to cook rice. Traditionally 1 cup white rice is cooked in 2 cups water or broth. A half teaspoon of salt is optional. Reduce or omit salt if broth is used. Some rice cookers come with their own measuring cup which contains less than a standard measuring cup. Rice cookers usually require 1/4 to 1/2 cup less water. Follow manufacturer's instructions carefully.

- Regular white rice takes 18 to 20 minutes. Makes 3 cups, 4 servings.
- Parboiled or converted white rice takes 20 to 25 minutes. Makes 4 cups, 4 to 6 servings.
- Brown rice takes 40 to 45 minutes. Use 2 1/2 cups liquid for each cup of rice. Makes 4 cups, 4 to 6 servings.
- Do not remove cover until all water is absorbed unless instructed otherwise in the recipe.
- Uncover when cooked and let dry out 3 to 5 minutes before serving. Fluff with a fork.
- One cup of rice generally serves 2 to 4 people depending on whether it is a side dish or main course.

Variations

- Cook favorite fresh herbs such as basil or thyme with rice or toss with steamed rice before serving.
- Toss with butter and toasted almonds when cooked.
- Mix steamed rice cooked in broth with mushrooms sautéed in butter.
- Add 1/8 teaspoon powdered saffron to cooking liquid. Season with salt and freshly ground black pepper.
- Add 2 tablespoons poppy or caraway seeds and melted butter. Season with salt and freshly ground black pepper.
- Add 1/8 cup minced pitted olives and 2 tablespoons olive oil.

- Add 1 coarsely chopped small avocado and ¹/₂ cup coarsely chopped peeled and seeded tomato.
- Add ¹/₄ cup minced fresh mint warmed for 3 minutes in 2 tablespoons butter.
- Add 1 cup sour cream. Sprinkle with 2 tablespoons minced chives.
- Add ¹/₂ cup freshly grated Parmesan cheese or mozzarella cheese.

Steamed Rice with Fresh Basil and Cheeses

Butter and cheese melting in a bowl of hot steamed rice is one of the joys of the Italian table. In this version rice is tossed with butter, fresh basil, freshly grated Parmesan cheese, and mozzarella.

3 cups hot steamed rice
2 tablespoons butter, at room temperature
4 ounces mozzarella, shredded
1/4 cup freshly grated Parmesan cheese
2 tablespoons minced fresh basil

Put hot rice in serving bowl. Mix in butter, mozzarella, and freshly grated Parmesan cheese. Add basil; fluff rice with fork before serving.

Serves 4

Herbed Rice

Fresh herbs add a delicate flavoring to steamed rice. Do not substitute dried herbs. The flavor will not be as good.

2 tablespoons minced fresh dill, basil, or chives
2 tablespoons butter or olive oil
1 cup uncooked rice
2 cups chicken broth
Salt to taste

Warm dill in butter or olive oil for 1 minute. Combine dill mixture with rice and chicken broth in steaming pan; season to taste. Cover and steam until rice is done, about 20 minutes. Fluff rice with fork before serving.

Serves 4

Variation

- Mix herbs, butter, rice, and water together in steaming pan instead of warming herbs in butter or olive oil first.

Brown Rice with Fresh Oregano and Mushrooms

Brown rice is high in nutrients. Sautéing it in olive oil or butter before steaming intensifies its nutty flavor.

2 tablespoons olive oil or butter
1 cup sliced mushrooms
2 tablespoons minced fresh oregano
1 cup brown rice
4 cups water
$^1/_2$ teaspoon salt (optional)

Sauté mushrooms and fresh oregano in olive oil or butter in nonstick pan for 1 minute. Remove from pan; reserve. Sauté rice in same pan, stirring constantly, until rice is well coated, about 2 minutes. Combine rice with water and salt in steaming pan; cover and steam until rice is done, 40 to 45 minutes. Toss reserved mushrooms with hot rice. Serve immediately.

Serves 4

Variations

- Any fresh herb such as basil, thyme, cilantro, or a combination can be used.
- For a nuttier texture, uncooked rice can also be toasted in a preheated 350°F oven. Spread rice on a cookie sheet and toast, stirring occasionally, 8 to 10 minutes until golden. Steam rice in the usual way.
- Vary ingredients as you would in any rice.

Basic Wild Rice

Especially good with game or poultry.

³/₄ cup wild rice
3 cups water
¹/₂ teaspoon salt (optional)
2 tablespoons butter or margarine, at room temperature

Combine wild rice, water, and salt in steaming pan; cover and steam until done, about 45 minutes. Add butter; fluff with fork before serving.

Serves 4

Variation

• Mix steamed wild rice with sautéed mushrooms and fresh herbs.

Pilaf

In Middle Eastern countries, the preparation of pilaf is considered an art. The preferred kind of rice used is a long grain white rice that will produce a light and fluffy pilaf with a firm texture, not a gummy or mashed consistency. The amount of liquid used in cooking rice is crucial in determining the final outcome. Too much liquid will produce a soggy result. Not enough will produce pilaf that is not fully cooked. With practice, you will gradually develop the ability to determine the exact amount of liquid needed to make pilaf in your rice cooker.

Traditionally, rice is sautéed in butter; olive oil is a healthful substitute that adds a different flavor to the finished dish. The amount of olive oil or butter used depends on the richness of the liquid. If water is used, more olive oil or butter is recommended. This step can be accomplished in some rice cookers, but not in the above-the-water type. It can be done in a separate nonstick pan before combining with the rice and seasonings. Or eliminate olive oil or butter by steaming the onion and/or garlic in water, chicken, or beef broth, or adding it uncooked to the steaming pan.

Pilaf is best prepared close to serving time. Rice should be tender but still firm to the bite, not mushy. A bed of plain rice pilaf complements all the kebabs, stews, and almost any meat course in Middle Eastern cookery. It is often served with yogurt.

Basic Pilaf

2 tablespoons olive oil or butter
1 cup uncooked rice
2 cups hot chicken or beef broth, or water
1/2 teaspoon salt (optional)

Sauté rice, stirring constantly, in hot oil or butter in nonstick pan until translucent, about 2 minutes. Combine rice and broth in steaming pan; season to taste. Cover and steam until the rice is done, 18 to 20 minutes. Uncover and allow to dry out, 3 to 5 minutes. Fluff with a fork before serving.

Serves 4

Variations

- Soak rice in hot water; allow to cool; drain and proceed with recipe. Turkish cooks consider this step necessary for a fluffier rice.
- Although not typical, pilaf may be flavored with onion and garlic.
- Pilaf may be sprinkled with finely chopped parsley or paprika to taste just before serving.
- Like their neighbors in Italy, Greeks love tomatoes so they sometimes add the flavor to pilaf. Sauté 1/2 cup finely chopped onion in oil. Add 1/2 cup finely chopped tomato or tomato sauce to rice and broth in steaming pan. Onion may be omitted.

Armenian Vermicelli Pilaf

This popular dish is used interchangeably with plain rice pilaf. Especially good with chicken and lamb stews.

1 cup uncooked rice
1/2 cup vermicelli, broken into 1-inch pieces
2 tablespoons olive oil or butter
2 cups chicken or beef broth
Salt to taste

Sauté rice and vermicelli, stirring constantly, in olive oil or butter in nonstick pan until rice is translucent, about 2 minutes. Combine rice and vermicelli with broth in steaming pan; season to taste. Cover and steam until rice is done, 18 to 20 minutes. Uncover and allow to dry out, 3 to 5 minutes. Fluff with a fork before serving.

Serves 4

Variations

- Turkish cooks sometimes chop and add the white parts of a few scallions at the end of the steaming step.
- Substitute 1/2 cup fine egg noodles for vermicelli.

Pilaf with Almonds

A nice contrast to roast turkey or chicken.

1 ½ teaspoons olive oil or butter
¼ cup blanched almonds
Salt to taste
1 cup uncooked rice
2 tablespoons olive oil or butter
2 cups chicken or beef broth
Salt to taste

Sauté almonds in olive oil or butter in nonstick pan until golden, stirring frequently. Drain on absorbent paper; sprinkle with salt. Reserve. Sauté rice, stirring constantly, in same pan with additional olive oil or butter until translucent, about 2 minutes.

Combine rice with broth in steaming pan; cover and steam until rice is done, 18 to 20 minutes. Uncover and allow to dry out, 3 to 5 minutes. Fluff with a fork before serving; top with sautéed almonds.

Serves 4

Golden Saffron Pilaf

A golden saffron rice with toasted almonds and sesame seeds often accompanies roasted fowl or meat on festive occasions in the Middle East.

1/4 cup sliced almonds
1/4 cup sesame seeds
1 cup uncooked rice
2 tablespoon olive oil or butter
2 cups chicken or beef broth
1/4 teaspoon powdered saffron
Salt to taste

Toast sliced almonds and sesame seeds on baking sheet in pre-heated 300°F oven until golden brown, stirring occasionally. Watch closely to prevent burning. Reserve.

Sauté rice, stirring constantly, in olive oil or butter in non-stick pan until translucent, about 2 minutes. Combine rice, broth, and saffron in steaming pan; season to taste. Cover and steam until rice is done, 18 to 20 minutes. Uncover; allow to dry out, 3 to 5 minutes. Use a fork to mix rice with toasted almonds and sesame seeds.

Serves 4

Variation

• Omit the toasted almonds and sesame seeds for plain saffron pilaf.

Dried Fruit Pilaf

Pilaf made with dried fruits is particularly good with roasted or barbecued pork or chicken.

1 cup uncooked rice
2 tablespoons butter or margarine
2 cups water

Sauce:

2 tablespoons butter or margarine
1/4 cup dried apricots
1/4 cup dried prunes
1/4 cup dried currants
1/4 cup finely chopped blanched almonds
2 tablespoons honey
1 tablespoon hot water

Sauté rice, stirring constantly, in nonstick pan with butter or margarine until translucent, about 2 minutes. Combine rice with water in steaming pan; cover and steam until rice is done, 18 to 20 minutes. Uncover and allow to dry out, 3 to 5 minutes.

Prepare sauce while rice is steaming. Sauté fruits and nuts in butter or margarine in nonstick pan until lightly browned, stirring frequently. Combine honey and water; add to pan. Simmer over low heat 10 minutes or until liquid is thickened, stirring occasionally.

Fluff hot pilaf with a fork before serving topped with fruit sauce.

Serves 4

Variation

- Make a date sauce by sautéing 1/2 cup slivered blanched almonds in butter or margarine. Add 1/2 cup *each* chopped dates and golden raisins. Cook, stirring frequently, 5 minutes. Stir in 1 tablespoon orange flower water or 1 teaspoon grated orange peel.

Chinese Rice Snack

Chinese children eat this unassuming dish after school. Leftover rice, at room temperature rather than cold, is mixed with oil and sprinkled with dark soy sauce and finely chopped scallions.

3 cups cooked rice, at room temperature
2 tablespoons peanut oil
3 tablespoons soy sauce
2 scallions with green tops, finely chopped

Add oil to rice; mix thoroughly. Add soy sauce; toss gently. (The oil and rice must be mixed first so that each grain is coated and soy sauce will distribute evenly.) Sprinkle with chopped scallions; fluff with fork.

Serves 4

Chinese Pork Fried Rice

This is probably the most popular Chinese dish in America. An excellent way to use leftover cooked rice as well as bits of meat, poultry, and vegetables.

2 tablespoons oil
1 small onion, diced
1 clove garlic, minced
1/3 cup sliced fresh mushrooms
6 water chestnuts, sliced
1/3 cup frozen peas, thawed and drained
3 cups cold cooked rice
1/2 cup diced cooked pork or chicken
Freshly ground black pepper to taste
2 tablespoons soy sauce
1 tablespoon oil
2 eggs, beaten
1 scallion with green top, finely chopped

Stir-fry onion and garlic in hot oil in nonstick pan until onion is limp and golden, about 2 minutes. Add mushrooms, water chestnuts, and peas; stir-fry 2 minutes more. Add rice and stir-fry until rice is hot and well mixed with vegetables. Add pork or chicken; season with black pepper and soy sauce. Cook, stirring, until hot.

Move rice to one side of pan; heat additional oil. Add beaten eggs; allow eggs to begin to set before blending with rice. When blended, add scallion; mix 1 minute. Serve immediately.

Serves 4

Japanese Fried Rice

It is important to use cold rice in fried rice. A short grain white rice is used in Japan.

2 tablespoons oil
1 egg, beaten
3 cups cold cooked rice
4 scallions with green tops, chopped
1/2 cup cooked shrimp or crabmeat
1/2 cup frozen green peas, thawed and drained
1 tablespoon soy sauce

Heat oil in nonstick pan; add egg and scramble briefly. Add rice, scallions, seafood, and green peas. Stir gently until hot, about 3 minutes. Add soy sauce; mix thoroughly before serving.

Serves 4

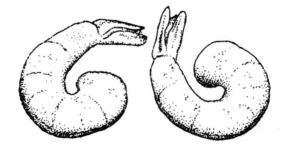

Indonesian Fried Rice

Indonesian fried rice is called *nasi goreng*. *Nasi* means "rice" and *goreng* means "fried."

3 tablespoons peanut oil
1 medium onion, chopped
2 cloves garlic, minced
3 cups cold cooked rice, cooked in chicken broth
1 cup julienned cooked chicken
1/2 cup diced ham
1/2 cup diced cooked shrimp
1/4 teaspoon ground cumin
1/4 teaspoon dried ground chile peppers
1/2 teaspoon ground coriander
1 tablespoon ground cashew nuts
2 tablespoons peanut butter

Sauté onions and garlic in hot oil in nonstick pan until limp. Stir in cooked rice; sauté until hot, stirring frequently. Mix in rest of ingredients. Cook over low heat 10 minutes, stirring occasionally.

Serves 4

Korean Honeyed Rice with Nuts

A touch of honey and nuts are combined with hot rice. Not a dessert.

1/2 cup blanched chopped almonds
1/4 cup pine nuts
2 tablespoons oil
4 cups hot cooked rice
3 tablespoons honey
1 1/2 tablespoons soy sauce

Sauté nuts in hot oil in nonstick pan until lightly browned. Add hot rice; mix with honey and soy sauce.

Serves 4

Indian Rice with Buttermilk

A cold rice made in India for picnics.

1 1/2 cups cold cooked rice
1 cup buttermilk
1 clove garlic, minced
1 teaspoon minced hot green chile pepper
1/4 cup chopped fresh cilantro
Salt to taste

Combine ingredients in bowl. Add more buttermilk if rice does
not hold together. Press into a pan; chill. Cut into squares and
serve cold.

Serves 4

West African Coconut Rice

Rice is cooked in coconut milk as is sometimes done in the Far East. The West African touch is the addition of tomatoes and onions.

2 cups coconut milk
1 teaspoon dried ground crayfish
1 cup uncooked rice
2 cups canned tomatoes, undrained
1 small onion, chopped
Salt to taste
Cayenne pepper to taste

Bring coconut milk to a boil. Combine rice, crayfish, tomatoes, and onions with coconut milk in steaming pan; season with salt and cayenne pepper to taste. Cover and steam until rice is quite dry, 18 to 20 minutes. Fluff with fork before serving. Adjust seasoning if necessary.

Serves 4

Variation

- To make coconut milk, cover fresh grated coconut with hot water (approximately 3 cups). Let soak 20 to 30 minutes. Place in colander; drain over a bowl, squeezing out as much liquid as possible. Makes about 2 cups. If not, add a bit more water to the grated coconut; drain again.

Hashed Brown Rice

This is as good as it is fast and easy to make. A crispy dish to serve with broiled steak or chicken.

3 cups cooked rice
3 tablespoons flour
1/4 cup milk
2 tablespoons olive oil
1/2 cup chopped onion
Salt and freshly ground black pepper to taste

Combine cooked rice, flour, and milk in bowl. Reserve. Sauté onion in olive oil in nonstick skillet until limp and golden. Mix rice mixture with onion; season with salt and pepper to taste. Press onion-rice mixture down firmly in skillet. (Pan should still be greased with oil. If not, add some.) Cook over medium heat until bottom is golden brown. Turn out onto serving dish, brown side up. Serve immediately.

Serves 4

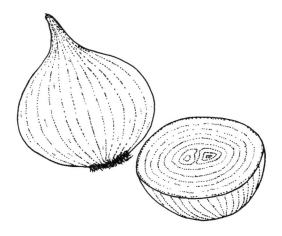

Mexican Rice

A spicy rice to serve with a simple meat loaf or hamburgers.

2 tablespoons olive oil
1 cup uncooked rice
1 small onion, minced
1/2 cup chopped green pepper
1 cup canned tomatoes, undrained
2 cups water
2 teaspoons chili powder or to taste
Salt to taste

Sauté rice in olive oil until translucent, about 2 minutes. Combine rice with onion, green pepper, tomatoes, and water in steaming pan; season with chili powder and salt to taste. Cover and steam until rice is done, 18 to 20 minutes. Uncover and allow to dry out, 3 to 5 minutes. Adjust seasoning if necessary. Fluff with a fork before serving.

Serves 4

Orange Rice

Agreeably pungent, orange rice is a perfect accompaniment for duck or other poultry.

2 tablespoons butter or margarine
2/3 cup sliced celery
2 tablespoons chopped onion
1 cup uncooked rice
1 1/2 cups water
1 cup orange juice
2 tablespoons grated orange peel
Salt to taste

Sauté celery and onion in butter until vegetables are limp. Combine celery-onion mixture with rice, water, orange juice, orange peel, and salt in steaming pan. Cover and steam until rice is done, 18 to 20 minutes. Uncover and allow rice to dry out, 3 to 5 minutes. Adjust seasoning if necessary. Fluff with a fork before serving.

Serves 4

Pacha Rice

An excellent rice and vermicelli dish from Egypt. Delicious with lamb kebabs or use as a poultry stuffing.

1/3 cup chopped, peeled almonds (or any favorite nut)
1/3 cup raisins, soaked in hot water and drained
2 tablespoons butter or olive oil
1 medium onion, finely chopped
1/2 pound chicken livers, finely chopped
1 clove garlic, minced
1/8 teaspoon saffron
Pinch of thyme
Pinch of coriander
Pinch of basil
Pinch of cayenne pepper
Salt and freshly ground black pepper to taste
1 cup uncooked rice
2 cups water
1/4 pound vermicelli, broken into 1-inch lengths
1 tablespoon oil

Prepare almonds and raisins. Reserve. Sauté onion and chicken livers in butter or olive oil in nonstick pan until onion is limp and chicken livers are lightly browned. Stir in garlic, saffron, thyme, coriander, basil, and cayenne pepper. Season with salt and pepper to taste. Combine with nuts, well-drained raisins, and rice in steaming pan. Add water; cover and steam rice until done, 18 to 20 minutes. Rice will be yellow and shiny.

Meanwhile, cook vermicelli in boiling water for 3 minutes. Drain; pour cold water over it. Drain thoroughly. Sauté well-drained vermicelli in hot oil for 5 minutes, turning gently. When rice is done, stir in vermicelli. Allow flavors to blend and rice to dry out, 3 to 5 minutes. Fluff rice with fork before serving.

Serves 4

Peanut Rice

The popular Southern name *goober* is from an African word for peanut, *nguba*. Delicious with chicken or ham.

3 cups cooked rice
1 cup finely chopped celery
1/2 cup finely chopped salted, skinless peanuts

Mix together rice, celery, and salted peanuts in nonstick pan. Cover and steam until hot, about 5 minutes. Add 1 to 2 tablespoons water if too dry.

Serves 4

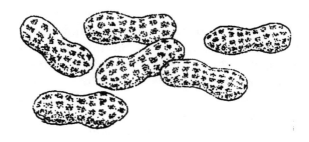

Spanish Saffron Rice

Saffron is an adaptation of the Arabic word *Za'faran* meaning "yellow." Saffron rice should have a fairly dry consistency.

2 tablespoons olive oil
1 cup uncooked rice
2 shallots, minced
2 1/2 cups chicken stock
1/2 teaspoon saffron
Salt and freshly ground black pepper to taste

Sauté rice and shallots in olive oil until shallots are limp. Combine rice and shallots with broth in steaming pan; season with saffron, salt, and pepper. Cover and steam until rice is done, 18 to 20 minutes. Uncover and allow to dry out, 3 to 5 minutes. Fluff with fork before serving.

Serves 4

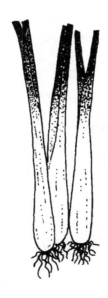

Spanish Rice

Highly seasoned rice topped with cheddar cheese is an excellent accompaniment for grilled steak or hamburgers.

1 slice bacon, chopped, or 2 tablespoons olive oil
1 small onion, minced
¼ cup chopped green pepper
¼ cup chopped celery
2 cups cooked rice
2 cups canned tomatoes, undrained and chopped
1 cup water
¼ teaspoon Worcestershire sauce
Salt to taste
1 cup shredded cheddar cheese

Fry bacon until crisp in nonstick pan. Remove bacon from pan and pour off drippings, leaving 1 tablespoon. Add onion, green pepper, and celery; brown lightly. Stir in rice, tomatoes, water, Worcestershire sauce, and salt to taste. Crumble bacon; stir into rice mixture. Sprinkle cheese over top. Cover and cook until cheese is melted, about 5 minutes.

Serves 4

Sushi

(Japanese Vinegared Rice)

Sushi rice is the Japanese equivalent of the open-faced American sandwich. Rice flavored with a vinegar-and-sugar dressing takes the place of bread, and is filled with various raw fish, pickles, mushrooms, or other vegetables. Use a short grain white rice if possible.

2 cups uncooked rice, washed and drained
3 cups water
1 (3-inch) piece of kombu (seaweed), washed under cold
　　running water (optional)

Dressing
$1/4$ cup rice wine vinegar, or 3 tablespoons mild white vinegar
$1/4$ cup sugar
1 teaspoon salt

Combine rice and water in steaming pan; let rice soak 30 minutes. Add kombu to rice (if available). Cover and cook until rice is done, about 20 minutes. Allow rice to rest 4 to 5 minutes. Place rice in shallow dish.

　　To make dressing, mix vinegar with sugar and salt. Pour over rice; mix lightly with a fork. Cool. Rice is ready to be used when it has reached room temperature.

Serves 6 to 8

Variations

- Rice with raw fish, rice rolled in seaweed, rice wrapped in omelette, rice in fried bean curd, and rice with seafood and vegetables are among the most popular types of sushi.
- To make fish balls, form 1 tablespoon of sushi rice into an oval. Place a slice of raw fish on top; mold it as symmetrically as possible. Sprinkle with sesame seeds. Serve with soy sauce.

Arroz Valenciana

The Spanish use saffron to color their delicious paella, but in Puerto Rico and many South American countries *achiote* (annatto seed) is used to color native rice dishes. Achiote is tasteless. The red coloring is obtained by slowly heating it in oil.

¹/₂ pound chorizo (Spanish sausage), cut in ³/₄-inch pieces
1 teaspoon achiote
4 cups hot cooked rice
1 cup frozen peas, thawed and drained
2 tablespoons slivered carrot
Salt and freshly ground black pepper to taste
4 hard-boiled eggs, shelled and quartered

Fry sausage until well cooked and browned. Remove sausage from pan; keep warm. If necessary, add enough oil to pan to make 2 tablespoons oil. Add achiote; cook until oil is red. Combine chorizo with rice, peas, and carrot in oil; mix, stirring frequently, until hot. Season to taste. Arrange quartered eggs on top and serve immediately.

Serves 4

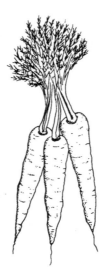

Curried Fruit on Rice

An unusual dish for a summer luncheon. Hot curry sauce is poured over sliced fruit and hot rice.

1 cup chicken broth
1 cup white wine
1 cup raisins
1 cup pine nuts
1 1/2 tablespoons curry powder
1 tablespoon cornstarch
Pinch of salt
1/4 cup chicken broth
1/4 cup white wine
4 cups hot cooked rice

Suggested Fruits

2 bananas, sliced
2 fresh peaches, sliced
4 slices pineapple
1/2 cup grated coconut

Combine 1 cup *each* chicken broth and wine in saucepan; bring to a boil. Add raisins and nuts; reduce heat and simmer 5 minutes. Mix curry powder with cornstarch, salt, and remaining broth and wine. Stir into simmering sauce. Cook, stirring constantly, until sauce thickens and clears. Adjust seasoning if necessary.

To serve, arrange fruit on top of hot rice. Pour hot curry sauce over the top. Sprinkle with coconut and serve.

Serves 4 to 6

Rice Cereal

Brown rice is especially good in this dish because of its nutty taste.

1 cup uncooked rice
2 cups water
$^1/_2$ teaspoon salt
2 tablespoons honey
$^1/_2$ cup pineapple juice
$^1/_2$ cup pineapple cubes
$^1/_2$ cup diced apricots or peaches
$^1/_2$ cup fresh seasonal berries or frozen sliced strawberries
Light cream

Combine rice, water, and salt in steaming pan; cover and steam until rice is tender, about 20 minutes. Add honey, pineapple juice, pineapple cubes, apricots, and berries to pan; cover for 7 to 8 minutes, until fruits are hot. Serve topped with light cream.

Serves 4

CHAPTER 3

Eggs and Cheese

*E*lectric egg cookers have been on the market for some time. They soft-boil, hard-boil, and poach eggs beautifully. The classic three-minute egg takes about five minutes while hard-boiled eggs cook in about twenty minutes.

Your electric rice cooker does the job just as easily with little of the cook's attention. Follow the manufacturer's instructions for perfect results every time. It is not worth the time involved to scramble eggs in a steamer.

Cheese is used in other recipes in this book, but in the ones gathered here the flavor of cheese is primarily responsible for the success of the dish.

Rice with Cheese

Simply delicious with anything.

4 cups hot cooked rice
3 tablespoons butter or margarine, at room temperature
2 tablespoons freshly grated Parmesan or Romano cheese
1/8 teaspoon freshly ground black pepper

Mix rice with butter, grated cheese, and black pepper with a fork until well blended. Serve immediately.

Serves 4

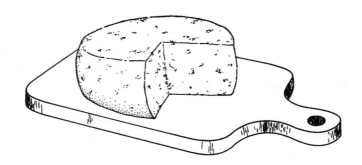

Rice with Lemon and Egg

Lemon adds zest to this simple dish. A good side dish with fish.

3 cups hot cooked rice
2 tablespoons butter or margarine
2 eggs, beaten
1/2 cup freshly grated Parmesan cheese
Juice of 1 lemon

Melt butter in nonstick pan; add cooked rice. Beat eggs, cheese, and lemon juice together; pour mixture into rice. Cook over low heat, stirring constantly, 3 to 4 minutes. Serve at once while rice is still creamy.

Serves 4

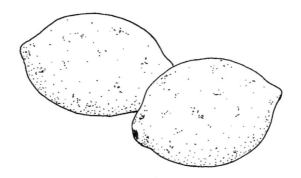

Risotto

The risotto technique exploits the uncommon properties of the Italian rice *arborio,* whose kernel is enveloped by a soft starch known as amylopectin. When it is subjected to appropriate cooking, that starch dissolves, creamily binding the kernels together and fusing them with the vegetables, meat, fish, or other ingredients. The resulting dish is *risotto.*

Long grain white rice will turn into a perfectly agreeable dish, but the "creamy" quality will be missing.

Virtually anything edible can become the flavor base of a risotto: cheese, fish, meat, vegetables, legumes, even fruit. In most instances, the ingredients of the base are put in before the rice. However, cheese goes in during the final stage of cooking, as do clams and mussels which must be protected from overcooking.

The risotto's base traditionally rests on a foundation of chopped onion sautéed in butter. If olive oil replaces the butter, garlic may be added.

Rice is sautéed in butter until it is translucent. Liquid is added to the pan and the rice is stirred until the liquid evaporates. More liquid is added and the procedure is repeated until the rice is done.

The quantity of liquid suggested in the recipes is approximate. In actual cooking, be prepared to use more, or sometimes less, as the risotto itself requires. If you have used up the broth before the rice is fully cooked, add hot water.

Some Italian cooks like the grains in risotto firm, and suggest cooking times of 18 to 20 minutes, and others cook the rice another 5 to 10 minutes. It is prudent to begin to taste the rice after 20 minutes cooking time so you can judge how much further it has to go, and how much more liquid to add, if any. Rice should be tender, but still firm to the bite.

Risottos can be grouped into two basic styles that differ in their consistency. The Piedmontese/Milanese/Bolognese style, compact and somewhat sticky, is founded on cheese, sausage, game, and wild mushrooms. The Venetian risotto known as *all'onda* is looser and achieves great delicacy with seafood and spring vegetables.

Unlike pasta, risotto tastes better when it has rested on your plate a minute or so.

Risotto alla Milanese

Risotto is to the north of Italy what pasta is to the south. This one is a classic—delicious with veal or chicken. Long grain white rice can be substituted if arborio rice is unavailable.

2 tablespoons butter or olive oil
1 small onion, finely chopped
1 clove garlic, minced
1 cup uncooked rice, preferably arborio
1/2 cup dry white wine
3 cups hot chicken broth
1/4 teaspoon powdered saffron
3 tablespoons freshly grated Parmesan cheese
2 tablespoons butter
Salt and freshly ground black pepper to taste

Sauté onion and garlic in butter or olive oil in nonstick pan until onion is limp and golden, about 2 minutes. Add rice; stir until translucent, about 2 minutes.

Add wine; cook, stirring constantly, until all the liquid is absorbed. Combine rice-onion mixture with 2 cups chicken broth in steaming pan. Stir once; cover and steam 18 to 20 minutes.

Five minutes before rice is done, dissolve saffron in rest of broth; stir rice, adding broth with grated cheese, butter, salt, and pepper to taste. Stop adding liquid when rice is tender with still a little "bite" to each grain. Rice should be slightly moist, but not runny.

Serves 4

Variations

- *Zucchini Risotto:* Sauté a sliced zucchini with the onion and garlic. Proceed as directed.
- *Mushroom Risotto:* Sauté 1/2 pound sliced mushrooms along with the onion and rice. Proceed as directed. Toss with 3/4 cup pine nuts and grated cheese.
- *Chicken Liver Risotto:* Sauté 1 pound chicken livers. Add onions and mushrooms. Proceed as directed.

Rice Croquettes

Croquettes are considered one of the specialties of fine French cooking, although this recipe comes from Italy. Croquettes go together better when the rice is still warm.

4 cups hot cooked rice, cooled slightly
3 tablespoons freshly grated Romano cheese
1 tablespoon minced fresh parsley
$1/8$ teaspoon freshly ground black pepper
2 to 3 medium eggs
Dry seasoned bread crumbs
Oil for frying

In large bowl mix together rice, cheese, parsley, and black pepper. Add 1 egg at a time until mixture sticks together.
Wet hands in oil or egg white; shape rice into oblong or round croquettes. Roll croquettes in bread crumbs.
     Heat $1/4$-inch oil in skillet; fry croquettes until golden brown all over. Drain on absorbent paper.

Variation

• Add cubed prosciutto, salami, or mozzarella in the center of each croquette for an extra surprise.

Baked Rice Pie

This is a marvelous recipe when you want to be very, very lazy after a busy day.

4 cups cooked rice
¹/₂ cup freshly grated Romano cheese
¹/₄ teaspoon freshly ground black pepper
2 eggs, beaten
1 teaspoon butter or margarine
¹/₂ pound mozzarella, cubed

In large bowl mix together rice, grated cheese, black pepper, and eggs. Put in a buttered 9-inch pie plate; top with cubed mozzarella. Bake for 20 minutes at 400°F. Slice and serve like a pie.

Serves 4

Variation

• Add chopped prosciutto or ham.

Cheese and Rice Soufflé

To achieve a perfect soufflé is not difficult with today's regulated and insulated ovens. Rice adds a nutlike texture to a cheese soufflé.

2 tablespoons butter or margarine
3 tablespoons flour
3/4 cup milk
1 cup coarsely grated cheddar cheese
4 egg yolks, beaten
1 cup cooked rice
4 egg whites, beaten until stiff

Mix flour into melted butter in saucepan; gradually add milk. Add cheese; cook, stirring constantly, until thickened. Add beaten egg yolks slowly to mixture, stirring constantly. Remove from heat; stir in rice. Cool slightly.

Beat egg whites until stiff. Gently fold into cheese-rice mixture. Turn into a greased 1 1/2-quart soufflé dish. Bake uncovered in a 325°F oven 35 to 40 minutes, until golden brown. Serve at once.

Serves 4 to 6

Baked Rice and Cheddar Cheese

There are many different types of cheddar cheese. Whether mild or sharp, moist or crumbly, they all have a recognizable common character. If you like macaroni and cheese, you should like this.

3 cups cooked rice
2 tablespoons butter or margarine
1/4 pound mild cheddar cheese, grated
2 cups milk
1 tablespoon minced fresh parsley
1 tablespoon grated onion
1/2 cup chopped ham
Salt and freshly ground black pepper to taste
Cracker crumbs

Mix together rice, butter, cheddar cheese, milk, parsley, onion, and ham. Season with salt and black pepper.

Pour into baking dish. Cover top with crumbs; bake at 350°F until brown and bubbly, about 20 minutes. Add more milk if dish becomes too dry.

Serves 4

CHAPTER 4

Vegetables

Vegetables are the best candidates for steaming, because nutrients are not leached out in cooking as they are by boiling. Steamed vegetables have a texture all their own. Just as a baked potato feels different in the mouth than a boiled potato, so does a steamed potato.

Steaming times in the recipes here are only guidelines. It takes practice to determine when vegetables are sufficiently cooked and not overdone. Times vary according to the size, freshness, and age of the vegetables, and how crowded the steamer is. Vegetables also take longer to cook if they are combined in a dish with meats or poultry.

The best way to steam vegetables is to place them directly on the steaming rack or basket an inch above the water. Don't overload the steamer. Test for doneness by piercing with a knife or skewer.

Some vegetables (potatoes and carrots among them) can take longer to steam than to boil. Green vegetables may lose their bright, vivid color and turn dull green. One way around this is to cook green vegetables such as brussels sprouts, broccoli, and green beans for shorter periods of time by cutting them into small pieces so they will cook before they change color. Remove vegetables from the steamer when they are still firm and immerse them immediately in cold water to halt the cooking process.

Dress steamed vegetables simply with fresh lemon or lime juice, or a light coating of lemon or lime butter sauce. Add color, texture, and/or flavor with minced fresh herbs such as basil, marjoram, oregano, and thyme, lightly toasted slivered nuts or sesame seeds, thin strips of sun-dried tomato, pimiento or roasted peppers, sliced pimiento-stuffed olives or sliced ripe olives, or freshly grated Parmesan, Romano, or other hard cheeses.

Steamed Broccoli

Steamed vegetables can be enhanced in myriad ways without losing important nutrients. Here's an example of what you can do with olive oil and garlic.

1 bunch fresh broccoli, prepared for steaming
2 tablespoons olive oil
2 cloves garlic, minced
Salt and freshly ground black pepper to taste

Using a paring knife, remove and discard the tough bottoms of the broccoli stalks, cut into florets, and slice stems. The smaller the pieces and less crowded the steaming basket is, the quicker the broccoli will cook.

Place broccoli in steamer basket; steam until tender, 4 to 8 minutes. Do not overcook. To arrest cooking, add or plunge steamed broccoli in cold water. If done early enough in the cooking process, it preserves the vivid color of green vegetables.

Dress steamed broccoli with olive oil, garlic, and salt and black pepper to taste. Allow flavors to blend for 10 minutes.

Serves 4

Variations

- Steam broccoli sprinkled with olive oil and garlic.
- Stir-fry quickly steamed broccoli and garlic in hot oil in non-stick pan, making sure not to burn the garlic. Season with salt and freshly ground black pepper to taste. Serve immediately.

Steamed Artichokes

Artichokes are the leafy buds from a plant resembling the thistle. They have grown in the vicinity of Naples since the fifteenth century.

4 medium artichokes, prepared for steaming
2 tablespoons olive oil
2 tablespoons minced fresh thyme
2 tablespoons minced fresh marjoram
Salt and freshly ground black pepper to taste

Rinse artichokes and remove tough outer leaves. Cut off stems so artichokes can stand upright in steamer; cut about 3/4 inch off top and trim tips off outside leaves.

Place artichokes in steamer basket. Sprinkle with oil, herbs, and salt and pepper to taste. Steam artichokes until very tender, about 45 minutes. Test by pulling out artichoke leaf. It should come out easily. Serve hot or cold.

Serves 4

Variations

- Serve with lemon wedges or lemon butter.
- Stuff artichokes before steaming. Mix together 1 1/2 cups stale bread crumbs, 2 tablespoons olive oil, 1 minced garlic clove, 3 tablespoons freshly grated Parmesan cheese, 1 tablespoon minced fresh parsley, and freshly ground black pepper to taste. Gently spread leaves apart and push stuffing down between leaves. Steam as directed.

Sicilian Artichokes with Rice

This simple sauce of tomatoes, artichokes, anchovies, and black olives tastes so good over rice.

2 tablespoons olive oil
1 medium onion, chopped
1 (10-ounce) package frozen artichoke hearts, thawed and
   drained
2 cups canned Italian plum tomatoes, undrained and chopped
1 tablespoon minced fresh basil
1 tablespoon minced fresh marjoram
Salt and freshly ground black pepper to taste
2 anchovies, chopped
8 black cured olives, pitted and chopped
4 cups hot cooked rice
1/2 cup freshly grated Romano cheese

Sauté onion in hot oil in nonstick pan until limp and golden. Add artichoke hearts; sauté, stirring frequently, 5 minutes. Stir in tomatoes, basil, marjoram, salt, and pepper; simmer 15 minutes. Add anchovies and olives; simmer 5 minutes. Serve over hot rice sprinkled with grated cheese.

Serves 4

Italian Cabbage with Rice

Cabbage came to North America via the French explorer Jacques Cartier, who planted it in Canada on his third voyage in 1541–42.

2 tablespoons olive oil, or 1 slice bacon, cut in $1/2$-inch pieces
2 cloves garlic, minced
1 (2-pound) Savoy cabbage, cleaned, cored, and cut into wedges
$1/2$ cup water
$1/8$ teaspoon freshly ground black pepper
4 cups hot cooked rice
$1/2$ cup freshly grated Parmesan cheese

If using bacon, fry until almost done but not yet crisp, or heat oil; add garlic and sauté briefly until limp. Combine with cabbage and water in steaming pan; season with black pepper. Cover and cook until cabbage is tender, 8 to 10 minutes. Add more water if necessary. Stir hot cooked rice into cabbage mixture. Mix with grated cheese. Adjust seasoning if necessary. Allow flavors to blend 10 minutes before serving.

Serves 4

Variation

• Steam cabbage with uncooked bacon or olive oil and garlic sprinkled on top. Combine with rice as directed.

Greek Spinach and Rice

Originating in southwestern Asia, spinach probably reached China around A.D. 647. It was unknown to ancient Greeks and Romans. Mint flavors this dish while tomato adds extra color.

2 tablespoons olive oil
1 large onion, finely chopped
2 tomatoes, cored and sliced
1 pound fresh spinach, washed and stemmed, or 1 (10-ounce) package frozen spinach, thawed and drained
1 cup uncooked rice
1 tablespoon minced fresh mint
Salt and freshly ground black pepper to taste
2 cups water

Sauté onions in hot oil in nonstick pan until limp and golden. Add tomatoes; simmer until sauce thickens slightly. Combine tomato-onion mixture with spinach, rice, mint, salt, pepper, and water in steaming pan; cover and steam until rice is done, 18 to 20 minutes.

Serves 4

Variations

- Add spinach when rice is almost done.
- Substitute 3 diced zucchini for spinach.
- Omit tomato if you wish.
- Instead of mint, add 1 tablespoon minced fresh thyme and 1 bay leaf when sautéing onions. Remove bay leaf before serving.

Chinese String Beans with Pork

String beans Chinese-style become the highlight of any meal.

1 pound fresh green beans, washed, stemmed,
    and cut in 2-inch pieces
2 tablespoons oil
1/4 pound ground pork, beef, or turkey
1 clove garlic, minced
1 tablespoon soy sauce
1 cup chicken broth
1 teaspoon dry sherry
1 teaspoon cornstarch
1/4 teaspoon sesame oil
4 cups hot cooked rice

Presteam string beans 1 to 2 minutes; plunge into cold water to stop cooking process. Drain on absorbent paper. Don't stir-fry until dry.

Stir-fry string beans in hot oil in nonstick pan until skins begin to brown. Remove green beans from pan; reserve. Drain oil, reserving 1 tablespoon. Stir-fry pork until lightly browned; add garlic for 30 seconds. Add reserved green beans, broth, and sherry. Mix cornstarch with broth; stir until sauce thickens slightly. Sprinkle with sesame oil. Serve with hot rice.

Serves 4

Variations

- Steam string beans, pork, and garlic sprinkled with soy sauce and sherry until tender. Sprinkle with sesame oil before serving.
- Sauté 1 minced garlic clove and 2 slices prosciutto, shredded, in 2 tablespoons olive oil. Toss with steamed string beans.

Hungarian String Beans and Rice

An exceptionally nourishing dish of braised green beans cooked with rice. Sour cream is added at the end. Perfect with steak or lamb chops.

2 tablespoons oil
1 medium onion, chopped
1 (10-ounce) package frozen string beans, thawed and drained
1 tablespoon minced fresh parsley
1 teaspoon paprika
Salt to taste
1 teaspoon vinegar
2 cups water
1 cup cooked rice
1/2 cup sour cream, at room temperature

Sauté onion in hot oil in nonstick pan until limp and golden. Stir in string beans, parsley, and paprika; season with salt to taste. Sauté 5 minutes, stirring constantly. Do not let string beans brown. Add vinegar and water to bean mixture; cover and simmer slowly, 15 to 20 minutes. Stir in rice; cover and simmer 5 minutes. Mix some of bean liquid into sour cream and slowly stir into pan. Simmer, stirring constantly, for 2 minutes. Serve hot.

Serves 4

Curried Peas and Rice

Curry powder is probably the world's earliest spice blend. Chopped pickles and fresh mint are added at the last minute to this dish from India.

2 tablespoons butter or margarine
2 medium onions, finely chopped
1 clove garlic, minced
1 tablespoon curry powder
1 bay leaf
2 cloves
1 cup uncooked rice
2 cups water
1 (10-ounce) package frozen peas, thawed and drained
Salt and freshly ground black pepper to taste
2 tablespoons chopped fresh mint
2 tablespoons chopped celery
2 small sweet-sour gherkins, chopped

Sauté onion and garlic in butter in nonstick pan. Sprinkle with curry powder; add bay leaf and cloves. Sauté mixture until onion is limp and golden. Add rice; stir until rice is translucent, about 1 minute. Combine rice mixture with water in steaming pan; cover and steam until rice is done, 16 to 18 minutes.

Stir in peas; season with salt and pepper; add hot water if too dry. Cover 3 to 4 minutes more until peas are tender. Dish should have a creamy consistency. Stir in mint, celery, and pickles. Serve hot.

Serves 4

Vegetable Curry

Curries are native to the Indies where they are mentioned as early as A.D. 477. The word, from *Tamil kari*, is recorded in the English language in the sixteenth century.

2 cloves garlic, minced
1 tablespoon grated fresh ginger
1 large onion, chopped
2 tablespoons butter or margarine
1 tablespoon curry powder
1 tablespoon ground cumin
2 teaspoons ground coriander
2 teaspoons turmeric
2 teaspoons paprika
Cayenne pepper to taste
2 cups canned tomatoes, undrained
$1/4$ cup diced peeled apple
$1/4$ cup raisins
3 cups chopped steamed vegetables of choice (cauliflower,
    winter squash, eggplant, or uncooked vegetables such as
    peas or mushrooms)
1 tablespoon lemon juice
2 tablespoons unsweetened coconut
$1/4$ cup unflavored yogurt
4 cups hot cooked rice

Sauté garlic, ginger, and onion in butter in nonstick pan until limp. Sprinkle with curry powder, cumin, coriander, turmeric, paprika, and cayenne; stir to combine flavors. Add tomatoes, apple, and raisins; simmer gently, stirring occasionally, until tomatoes cook down and apple has melted into mixture, about 10 minutes. Add vegetables of your choice; stir well to coat with curry sauce. Simmer gently 10 minutes. Remove from heat.

Stir in lemon juice, coconut, and yogurt; adjust seasoning if necessary. Serve with hot rice

Serves 4

Thai Vegetable Curry

The subtle, nutty flavor of any of the aromatic rices such as jasmine enhances the flavor of this dish.

2 (14-ounce) cans coconut milk
2 tablespoons red curry paste
1/2 cup chicken or vegetable broth
4 tablespoons fish sauce (*nam pla*)
2 tablespoons brown sugar
1 zucchini, sliced
1/2 cup fresh snow peas, trimmed, or frozen snow peas,
    thawed and drained
1/2 cup sliced fresh mushrooms
1 (8-ounce) can sliced bamboo shoots, rinsed and drained
Fresh cilantro
4 cups hot cooked rice

Bring to boil 4 ounces coconut milk, curry paste, broth, fish sauce, and sugar in saucepan. Lower heat and simmer 10 minutes. Add zucchini, snow peas, mushrooms, bamboo shoots, and remaining coconut milk. Simmer until vegetables are tender, about 10 minutes. Garnish with fresh cilantro. Serve with hot rice.

Serves 4

Variation

• For a lighter curry, use 1 can coconut milk, increasing the amount of chicken or vegetable broth used.

Hoppin' John

Here is an easy version of this Southern favorite which features black-eyed peas, salt pork, and rice. Substitute olive oil for the traditional salt pork if you wish.

1/4 cup diced salt pork, or 2 slices bacon, diced, or
    2 tablespoons olive oil
1 (10-ounce) package frozen black-eyed peas,
    thawed and drained
3 cups cooked rice
Salt and freshly ground black pepper to taste
Crushed red pepper or Tabasco sauce to taste

If using salt pork, fry until brown and crisp in nonstick pan. Otherwise, heat oil; add peas, rice, salt, black pepper, and red pepper. Cover and cook until flavors are blended, about 10 minutes. Stir occasionally.

Serves 4

Variation

• Add cubed ham.

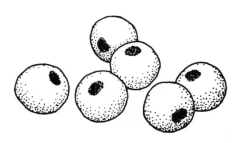

Italian Chick-Peas and Rice

Also known as garbanzo beans, Spanish beans, or ceci, chick-peas are one of the most nutritious legumes. This dish is good with fish or pork.

3 tablespoons olive oil
2 large onions, chopped
2 cups hot cooked rice
1 (15-ounce) can chick-peas, rinsed and drained
Salt and freshly ground black pepper to taste

Sauté onions in hot oil in nonstick pan until limp and golden. Add cooked rice, chick-peas, salt, and black pepper to taste. Sauté, stirring constantly, until mixture becomes dry like fried rice.

Serves 4

Variations

- Cooked black beans or lentils can be substituted for chick-peas.
- Crushed red pepper and/or chopped parsley are nice additions.

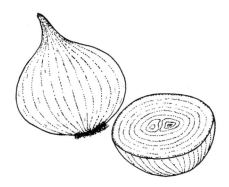

Japanese Red Beans and Rice

This combination of red beans and rice is a favorite dish of the Japanese. *Mochigome*, a glutinous-type rice, is used with azuki, Japanese red beans, but regular white rice and red kidney beans can be used.

1 cup uncooked rice
$1/2$ teaspoon salt
$1 1/2$ cups water
1 (15-ounce) can red kidney beans, washed and drained
3 tablespoons sake
3 tablespoons toasted sesame seeds

Put rice, water, and salt in steamer pan. Cover and steam until rice is tender, about 20 minutes. Add beans and sake to rice; mix together lightly with fork. Cover for 3 to 4 minutes. Mixture should be quite dry. Serve cold, sprinkled with toasted sesame seeds.

Serves 4

Variation

- To make Korean Beans and Rice, sauté 1 small chopped onion and 1 minced garlic clove in 2 tablespoons oil. Puree with 1 (15-ounce) can kidney beans, rinsed and drained, and 1 cup water in electric blender. Sauté mixture in 2 tablespoons oil. Stir in 2 cups cooked rice, $1/2$ cup beef broth, and $1/4$ teaspoon dried ground chile peppers.

Skillet Rice and Zucchini

Pretty and so good! Sautéed zucchini and onion are tossed with cooked rice and flavored with freshly grated Parmesan cheese.

2 tablespoons olive oil
1 medium onion, chopped
2 medium zucchini, sliced
1/2 teaspoon crushed red pepper
2 cups cooked rice
1/4 teaspoon freshly grated black pepper
1 scallion with green top, minced
1/4 cup chopped fresh parsley
1/2 cup freshly grated Parmesan cheese

Sauté onion, zucchini, and red pepper in olive oil in nonstick pan until onion is limp and golden, stirring occasionally. Stir in cooked rice and black pepper; cover for 3 to 4 minutes until hot. Toss scallion, parsley, and grated cheese with zucchini-rice mixture. Serve hot.

Serves 4

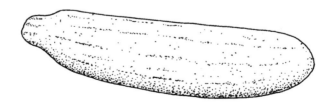

Thai Vegetable Stir-Fry

Thai food is becoming more and more popular in this country. This dish is easy enough for every day.

3 tablespoons peanut oil
1/4 cup sliced canned bamboo shoots, washed and drained
1/4 cup fresh snow peas, trimmed, or 1/4 cup frozen snow peas, thawed and drained
1 green bell pepper, cored, seeded, and thinly sliced
2 cloves garlic, minced
2 tablespoons fish sauce (*nam pla*)
4 tablespoons peanut satay sauce
1 tablespoon sugar
1/2 pound tofu, cubed
4 cups cooked rice

Stir-fry bamboo shoots, snow peas, and green pepper in hot oil in nonstick pan 2 to 3 minutes; add garlic for the last 30 seconds. Stir in fish sauce; cook, stirring constantly, 2 to 3 minutes. Add satay sauce, sugar, and tofu; cook until vegetables are done, 3 to 5 minutes. Serve with hot rice.

Serves 4

Variation

• Substitute sliced or cubed chicken for tofu. Adjust cooking time accordingly.

Tomato Pilaf

This is a popular base for making other pilafs, but it is often served as is. In the Middle East long grain white rice is soaked in hot water first for a fluffier rice.

2 tablespoons butter or olive oil
1 small onion, diced
1 clove garlic, minced (optional)
2 tomatoes, cored, seeded, and diced
2 tablespoons minced fresh basil
2 tablespoons minced parsley
Salt and freshly ground black pepper to taste
1 cup uncooked rice
1 1/2 cups hot chicken or beef broth, or water

Sauté onion and garlic in butter in nonstick pan until limp and golden. Add tomatoes, basil, and parsley; season with salt and pepper. Simmer until thick, about 10 minutes. Combine rice and broth with tomato mixture in steaming pan. Stir once; cover and steam until rice is done, 18 to 20 minutes.

Serves 4

Variations

- When onion is sautéed, add 1 cup sliced fresh mushrooms and 1 small green pepper, cored, seeded, and chopped. Add 1/4 teaspoon powdered saffron with broth. Sprinkle pilaf with 2 tablespoons minced fresh parsley when served.
- Rinse and drain a can of chick-peas; sauté in 2 tablespoons butter or olive oil. Stir into tomato pilaf 3 to 4 minutes before pilaf is done.

Italian Baked Eggplant and Rice Casserole

Casseroles are not supposed to be as good as this one! It features sautéed eggplant, peppers, and onions layered with rice and tomato sauce.

2 tablespoons olive oil
1 medium eggplant, stemmed and cubed
1 green pepper, cored, seeded, and chopped
1 medium onion, chopped
3 cups favorite tomato sauce
4 cups cooked rice (undercook slightly in chicken broth)
1/2 cup freshly grated Romano cheese

Sauté eggplant, pepper, and onion in 2 tablespoons olive oil in nonstick pan until lightly browned, about 10 minutes. In a 9 × 9 × 2-inch pan, layer rice, vegetable mixture, tomato sauce, and grated cheese alternately until ingredients are used, ending with rice, sauce, and cheese on top. Bake in 350°F oven until hot and bubbly, about 20 minutes

Serves 4

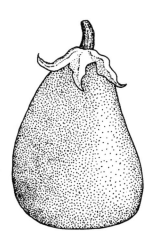

Risotto with Sun-Dried Tomatoes

Risotto is creating quite a stir in the United States these days, as are sun-dried tomatoes. Butter is traditional in risotto, but olive oil can be used.

2 tablespoons olive oil
3 scallions, minced
Salt and freshly ground black pepper to taste
1 cup uncooked rice, preferably arborio
1/4 cup chopped sun-dried tomatoes, packed in olive oil
1/2 cup dry white wine
3 cups chicken or vegetable broth
1 cup frozen peas, thawed and drained
1/4 cup freshly grated Parmesan cheese

Sauté scallions in olive oil in nonstick pan until limp. Season with salt and black pepper to taste. Add rice and sun-dried tomatoes; sauté, stirring constantly, until rice is translucent. Add wine, stirring frequently, until wine is almost absorbed.

Combine rice-tomato mixture with broth in steaming pan. Stir once; cover and steam until rice is almost done, 16 to 18 minutes. Stir in peas; add hot water if too dry. Rice should be creamy. Cover and steam 3 to 4 minutes. Serve with extra grated cheese.

Serves 4

Asparagus Risotto

Thomas Jefferson grew asparagus in his greenhouses at Monticello. It is one of the most popular vegetables in the United States today. Whatever vegetable is in season can be used in this superbly simple risotto.

3 tablespoons butter or margarine
1 small onion, thinly sliced
1 cup uncooked rice, preferably arborio
1 pound fresh asparagus, cleaned and cut in 2-inch pieces, or
    1 (10-ounce) package frozen asparagus, thawed and drained
3 1/2 cups chicken or vegetable broth
Freshly ground black pepper to taste
1/2 cup freshly grated Parmesan cheese
1 tablespoon butter, at room temperature.

Sauté onion in melted butter until limp and golden. Add rice and asparagus stalks, reserving tips. Stir until rice is translucent, about 1 minute. Add 1 cup stock, stirring constantly until broth is almost absorbed.

Combine rice mixture with rest of broth in steaming pan. Stir once; cover and steam until rice is done, 16 to 18 minutes. Stir in reserved asparagus, grated cheese, and butter. Rice should be creamy; add more broth if necessary.

Cover and allow flavors to blend 3 to 4 minutes before serving.

Serves 4

Artichoke Risotto

French settlers brought artichokes to Louisiana in the eighteenth century. Today they are mainly cultivated in the mid-coastal regions of California.

3 tablespoons olive oil
2 tablespoons minced onion
1 cup uncooked rice, preferably arborio
1 (10-ounce) box frozen artichoke hearts, thawed and drained
3 cups chicken or vegetable broth
2 tablespoons minced fresh basil
2 tablespoons minced fresh oregano
Salt and freshly ground black pepper to taste
3 tablespoons freshly grated Parmesan cheese
2 tablespoons minced fresh parsley
4 lemon wedges

Sauté onion in olive oil in nonstick pan until limp and golden. Add rice and artichoke hearts; sauté until rice is translucent. Add 1 cup broth, stirring constantly until broth is almost absorbed.

Combine rice mixture with remaining broth, basil, oregano, and salt and black pepper to taste in steaming pan. Cover and steam until rice is done, 16 to 18 minutes. Stir once; add more broth if too dry. Toss with Parmesan cheese and parsley before serving. Serve with additional cheese and lemon wedges.

Serves 4

Stuffed Vegetables

Steamed, stuffed vegetables served with a tossed salad and good bread make an easy do-ahead meal. Create your own fillings according to what you have on hand and/or your favorite flavor combinations.

Leftover brown, white, and wild rice can form the basis of fillings. Cooked meats, poultry, and sausage; chopped tomato or tomato sauce; small amounts of steamed vegetables; chopped green onion; minced pimiento; chopped nuts; grated cheese; fresh herbs; and lemon juice are only a few foods that can be used.

Dolma means "stuffed food" in the Middle East. Meat dolmas incorporate ground lamb or beef, rice or coarse bulghur, tomatoes, onions, herbs, seasonings, and occasionally nuts and currants. They are served hot as main dishes. Meatless dolmas are based on olive oil and are filled with a mixture of rice, tomatoes, onions, herbs, seasonings, nuts, and currants. They are served cold as appetizers or side or main dishes.

Dolmas are stuffed vegetables or fruits, simmered in broth or water, and flavored with lemon juice and sometimes tomatoes. *Sarmas* are stuffed leaves (grapevine, cabbage, and chard are the most common) cooked the same way. Both may be prepared with or without meat. Sarmas are sometimes referred to as dolmas.

Italian Stuffed Mushrooms

Large mushroom caps are filled with a delicate bread stuffing.

12 large mushrooms, cleaned
2 slices stale white bread, grated
3 tablespoons olive oil
3 tablespoons freshly grated Parmesan cheese
1 clove garlic, minced
1 tablespoon minced fresh parsley
1 tablespoon minced fresh basil
Pinch of freshly ground black pepper
Pinch of oregano

Clean mushrooms by wiping with damp cloth. Remove stems;
reserve for use in another dish. Mix together bread crumbs, olive
oil, grated cheese, garlic, parsley, basil, black pepper, and
oregano. Stuff mushroom caps; place in a single layer in steaming basket. Cover and steam until done, 7 to 8 minutes.

Serves 4

Pork and Rice Stuffed Acorn Squash

Acorn squash is a native American vegetable. The word squash comes from the Massachusetts Indian word *asquash* which means "eaten green." If squash is too big to steam, bake it.

2 small acorn squash, halved and seeded
2 cups ground sausage or turkey
1 medium onion, minced
2 cups cooked rice
Salt and freshly ground black pepper to taste
2 tablespoons freshly grated Parmesan cheese

Presteam squash, about 3 minutes. Drain and reserve.
Meanwhile, sauté sausage and onion in nonstick pan until well browned. (If ground turkey is used, add a little oil.) Mix rice, salt, black pepper, and cheese with sausage. Stuff squash with mixture; place squash in steaming basket. Cover and steam until tender, 15 to 20 minutes.

Serves 4

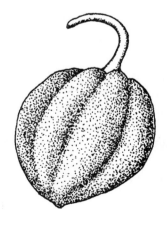

Chinese Stuffed Zucchini

Zucchini should be tender, not crunchy and not mushy. This is an inexpensive summer meal when zucchini are so plentiful.

3 medium zucchini, about 2 inches in diameter
1 scallion with green top, chopped
$1/2$ pound ground pork, beef, or turkey
1 egg
2 tablespoons sherry
1 teaspoon soy sauce

Sauce
1 cup chicken broth
1 teaspoon soy sauce
2 tablespoons dry sherry
2 tablespoons oyster sauce
1 tablespoon black bean sauce
1 tablespoon cornstarch
Water

Peel zucchini lengthwise in alternating strips with vegetable peeler; cut crosswise into $1^1/_2$-inch sections. Scoop out pulp from one side only of each section without going through the bottom. Reserve sections.

Mix together meat, egg, sherry, and soy sauce. (Refrigerate or mix 1 teaspoon cornstarch into mixture if too wet.) Stuff each section with filling. Place in steamer basket; cover and steam until done, 15 to 20 minutes.

To make sauce, combine broth, soy sauce, sherry, oyster sauce, and black bean sauce in saucepan; bring to boil. Lower heat; thicken with 1 tablespoon cornstarch mixed with water. Pour sauce over cooked zucchini; sprinkle with chopped scallions before serving immediately.

Serves 4

Variations

- Sprinkle before steaming with 1 teaspoon soy sauce, 1 table-spoon *each* sherry, oyster sauce, and black bean sauce. Sprinkle with choppped scallions before serving.
- Sprinkle flour on meat side of zucchini sections.Sauté zucchini sections, filling side down, until lightly browned, about 5 minutes. Turn and brown other side, about 3 minutes. Steam as directed.

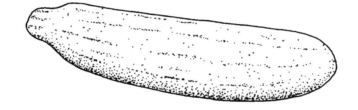

Greek Stuffed Tomatoes

Hard-to-please vegetarian friends will love this.

4 medium firm tomatoes
1 large onion, grated
2 tablespoons olive oil
1 1/2 cups cooked rice
2 tablespoons chopped fresh parsley
2 tablespoons chopped fresh dill
1 tablespoon raisins
1 tablespoon pine nuts
2 tablespoons olive oil

Wash tomatoes; cut off tops (do not sever so you can use as lids). Scoop out pulp and discard. Reserve tomatoes. Sauté onion in olive oil in nonstick pan until limp and golden. Mix rice, parsley, dill, raisins, and nuts with onion mixture. Stuff tomatoes with rice mixture; sprinkle with olive oil. Top with tomato caps; place tomatoes in steaming basket. Cover and steam until done, about 10 minutes. Serve cold.

Serves 4

Variations

- Use fresh mint instead of dill, or a combination of both.
- Use zucchini, peppers, and other vegetables instead of tomatoes.
- Sicilians stuff tomatoes with a bread crumb stuffing. Prepare tomatoes for stuffing in the same manner. After chopping and sautéing 1 small onion and 1 garlic clove in 2 tablespoons olive oil, add tomato pulp, 4 anchovies, 1 tablespoon capers, 1 cup fresh bread crumbs, salt and pepper to taste.

Greek Stuffed Grapevine Leaves

(Dolmadakia)

An excellent appetizer.

2 tablespoons olive oil
2 medium onions, finely chopped
1 ¹/₂ cups cooked rice
2 tablespoons olive oil
2 teaspoons minced fresh mint
2 teaspoons minced fresh dill
3 tablespoons minced fresh parsley
1 bunch scallions with tops, finely chopped
Salt and freshly ground black pepper to taste
Juice of 1 large lemon
1 (8-ounce) jar grapevine leaves, washed and drained
2 tablespoons olive oil

Place onions and olive oil in steaming pan; cover and steam until onions are limp, about 3 minutes. Mix onion mixture thoroughly with rice, olive oil, mint, dill, parsley, scallions, salt and pepper, and half the lemon juice.

After washing grapevine leaves thoroughly to remove brine, cut large leaves in half. Place 1 tablespoon filling on underside of leaf. Starting at base, fold over, and fold in sides, rolling tightly toward point. Arrange rolls in circles, making more than one layer, if necessary, in steaming basket. Sprinkle with olive oil and lemon juice. Cover and steam until tender, about 20 minutes. Serve cold sprinkled with lemon juice.

Serves 24

Variation

• Turkish recipes include tomato and currants.

Lamb Stuffed Peppers

Capers and black olives are the secret ingredients.

4 large green peppers, tops removed and seeded
2 tablespoons olive oil
1 small onion, minced
1 cup coarsely ground cooked lamb
1 1/2 cups cooked rice
1 cup tomato sauce
1 egg, beaten
3 tablespoons freshly grated Parmesan cheese
Salt and freshly ground black pepper to taste
1/8 teaspoon oregano
1/4 cup bread crumbs
1 tablespoon capers, drained
2 tablespoon black olives, sliced

Presteam peppers, about 2 minutes. Plunge into cold water; drain and reserve. Sauté onion in olive oil in nonstick pan until limp and golden. Stir in lamb for 1 minute; remove from heat. Mix lamb mixture with rice, tomato sauce, egg, grated cheese, salt and pepper, oregano, bread crumbs, capers, and black olives.

Stuff green peppers with mixture; place peppers in steaming basket. Cover and steam until peppers are tender, about 15 minutes.

Serves 4

Variations

- Combine lamb and rice with onion as directed. Add ¹/₂ cup minced fresh herbs, a mixture of savory, cilantro, mint, basil, and marjoram, or a combination of parsley, dill, and coriander. Salt and pepper to taste.
- For seafood lovers, stuff peppers with 2 cups chopped cooked shrimp or any leftover seafood mixed with 1 minced small onion, 2 tablespoons olive oil, 1 teaspoon Worcestershire sauce, 1 cup tomato sauce, 1¹/₂ cups cooked rice, and salt and black pepper to taste.
- Stuff peppers or any suitable vegetable with pilaf. Serve with Garlic Yogurt Sauce (see recipe on page 102).

Greek Stuffed Cabbage

No collection of stuffed vegetables would be complete without this famous Greek stuffed cabbage served in a delicate egg-lemon sauce.

1 (1 1/2-pound) cabbage
3/4 pound ground beef or turkey
1 medium onion, grated
1 tablespoon chopped fresh parsley
1 tablespoon chopped fresh mint
2 large tomatoes, chopped, or 1 (8-ounce) can tomatoes, undrained
1 small zucchini (optional)
1/2 teaspoon salt
2 tablespoons melted butter or olive oil
1/8 teaspoon freshly ground black pepper
1 1/2 cups cooked rice

Sauce

2 cups chicken broth
2 eggs
Juice of 1 lemon, or 2 ounces lemon juice

Cut core out of cabbage with a **V** cut. Steam until you can separate leaves with a knife and fork, about 5 minutes. Cut large leaves in half before stuffing.

To make filling, mix meat, onion, parsley, mint, tomatoes, zucchini, salt, butter or olive oil, black pepper, and rice together in bowl.

To stuff, form 1 tablespoon into a tiny hot dog; place on cabbage leaf on wider edge. Roll toward point; tuck in sides and finish rolling.

Place in steaming basket in circles. Cover and steam until tender, about 20 minutes.

To make Avgolemono (egg-lemon) sauce: Heat chicken broth in saucepan. Beat eggs and lemon juice together. Add a little broth to warm the egg mixture, stirring constantly. Adjust seasoning if necessary. Pour over steamed cabbage in serving dish. Allow to set 2 to 3 minutes before serving.

Serves 4

Variations

• Stew stuffed cabbage in chicken broth instead of steaming. Add water and bouillon cubes if more liquid is needed to cover cabbage rolls.

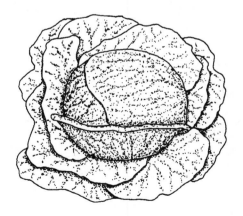

Garlic Yogurt Sauce

This is excellent with vegetable dolmas and some meat dolmas. It also complements fried eggplant or zucchini.

1 cup plain yogurt
1 medium clove garlic, or to taste
1/4 teaspoon salt
2 tablespoons fresh mint

Put yogurt into bowl. Pound garlic with salt and mint. Add to yogurt; mix well. Cover; chill several hours before serving.

CHAPTER 5

Seafood

*L*ike vegetables, fish retains more of its taste and delicate texture when it is steamed. Steaming also supplies extra moisture for lean fish, preventing it from overcooking and drying out.

Firm white-fleshed fish steam best. Good choices are sea bass, red snapper, whiting, salmon, flounder, cod, and tilefish. Oily fish such as bluefish and mackerel tend to become soft and break apart.

Steaming fish with favorite fresh herbs such as basil, dill, savory, thyme, rosemary, mint, and tarragon as well as more unusual herbs such as lemon balm, fennel (leaves), lovage, and cilantro provides innumerable flavor combinations. Before fish is steamed, the flesh is translucent. When done, the flesh will be opaque or milky. Steam fish in a pan and save juices for a natural sauce.

Fish cooks quickly and can be easily ruined by overcooking. As a rule of thumb, allow nine to ten minutes for each inch of thickness. Cooking time may need to be increased if there are other ingredients in the pan. Don't forget to adapt to the individual peculiarities of your electric rice cooker/steamer.

Steamed Halibut with Lemon

Easy and delicious. Fillets that are at least ¹/₂ inch thick steam best. Use steaming pan instead of steaming basket, and juices are preserved for a sauce.

1 pound halibut fillets, at least ¹/₂-inch thick,
   or any firm white fish
2 tablespoons soy sauce
Freshly ground black pepper to taste
1 lemon, thinly sliced

Place fish in a single layer in steaming pan. Sprinkle with soy sauce and pepper to taste. Top with lemon slices. Steam until fish is opaque and flakes easily with a fork, about 10 minutes.

Serves 2 to 4

Variations

- If steamer space is limited, try coiling fillet loosely.
- Sprinkle fish with 2 tablespoons olive oil, 2 minced garlic cloves or 1 small onion, thinly sliced, ¹/₈ teaspoon oregano, pinch of freshly ground black pepper, and 1 tablespoon minced fresh parsley. Steam as directed.

Chinese Steamed Sea Bass

To serve Chinese style, serve fish whole, including the head. (If you prefer, you may remove the head before steaming the fish.)

1- to 2-pound sea bass, split and cleaned (head and
   tail optional)
1 teaspoon minced fresh ginger
1 scallion with green top, chopped
1 teaspoon fermented black beans, rinsed and chopped
1 tablespoon soy sauce
1 tablespoon dry sherry
1 tablespoon peanut oil

Dry cleaned fish inside and outside. Place fish in steaming pan. Mix together ginger, scallion, black beans, soy sauce, dry sherry, and oil; pour over fish. Cover and steam until fish is opaque and flakes easily with fork, 15 to 20 minutes.

Serves 2 to 4

Variation

- Fine-textured fish such as porgy, trout, butterfish, flounder, sole, and whitefish can be steamed in the same way. Fillets of any of these fish can be used.

Steamed Red Snapper with Ginger and Basil

The word *basil* comes from the Greek word meaning "royal" or "king." Basil, which belongs to the mint family, is especially good with seafood.

1 pound red snapper fillets, at least 1/2-inch thick, or any firm white fish
2 tablespoons fermented black beans, rinsed and chopped
1 small fresh red chile pepper, seeded and finely chopped
2 teaspoons minced fresh ginger
1 clove garlic, minced
2 scallions with green tops, minced
2 tablespoons dry white wine
1 tablespoon peanut oil
1 tablespoon soy sauce
Fresh cilantro
1/2 cup minced fresh basil

Place fillets in steaming pan. Combine beans with chile pepper, ginger, garlic, and scallions. Spread mixture over fish. Sprinkle with wine, oil, soy sauce, and cilantro. Cover and steam until fish flakes easily with fork, about 10 minutes. Sprinkle with fresh basil and serve.

Serves 2 to 4

Variations

- Sprinkle fish with a simple topping of 2 tablespoons *each* fresh chopped basil, fennel leaves, and parsley before steaming.
- Serve steamed fish with fresh basil pesto. Blend 1 cup fresh basil and 1 clove garlic into a paste. Add 1/4 cup pine nuts and 1/4 cup freshly grated Parmesan cheese; process until smooth. With blender running, add 1/3 cup olive oil. Mix until smooth and creamy. Makes 3/4 cup.

Steamed Salmon with Mustard Dill Sauce

Ever popular steamed salmon is served with a pungent mustard dill sauce.

1 pound salmon steaks (about 4 ounces each)
1/4 cup dry white wine
2 tablespoons chopped fresh dill

Sauce

3 tablespoons Dijon-style mustard
2 tablespoons sugar
1 1/2 tablespoons white wine vinegar
1/4 cup vegetable oil
1/4 cup sour cream
1/4 cup chopped fresh dill

Place salmon steaks in steaming pan. Add wine and chopped fresh dill. Cover and steam until fish flakes easily with fork, about 10 minutes.

To make Mustard Dill Sauce, combine mustard, sugar, and vinegar in blender; blend until smooth. With motor running, add oil until mixture is thick. Stir in sour cream and fresh dill. Makes 1 cup.

Serve steaks plain or with Mustard Dill Sauce.

Serves 4

Steamed Halibut and Vegetables

Marinated halibut is rolled and steamed on a bed of vegetables.

4 halibut fillets, at least 1/2 inch thick, or any firm white fish
3 tablespoons soy sauce
3 tablespoons dry sherry
1 tablespoon minced onion
1/2 teaspoon sugar
1 1/2 teaspoons minced fresh ginger
1 large carrot, cut in 2-inch strips
1 medium zucchini, cut in 2-inch strips
2 scallions with green tops, minced
1 tablespoon soy sauce

Combine soy sauce, sherry, onion, sugar, and ginger in bowl. Marinate fish in mixture for 10 minutes. Place carrot and zucchini in single layer in steaming pan. Spread fillets out flat; sprinkle 2 tablespoons of scallions over fish. Roll up jelly-roll fashion. Place, seam side down, on vegetables. Cover and steam until fish is opaque and flakes easily with fork, about 15 minutes. Sprinkle with remaining scallions.

Serves 4

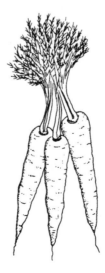

Swordfish Almandine

Almonds have been cultivated since antiquity in Mediterranean countries and the Orient. In the United States, they are grown commericially in California.

4 swordfish steaks (4 ounces each), or any firm white fish
3 tablespoons soy sauce
1 tablespoon vegetable oil
2 teaspoons sugar
$^1/_2$ teaspoon grated lime peel
2 teaspoons lime juice
$^1/_4$ cup toasted sliced almonds

Combine soy sauce, oil, sugar, lime peel, and juice; pour over fish. Refrigerate 1 hour.

Remove fish from marinade; place in steaming dish. Cover and steam until fish flakes easily with fork, about 10 minutes. Remove to serving dish; top with almonds.

Serves 4

Clam-Stuffed Flounder Rolls

An excellent clam-rice stuffing makes this simple-to-make dish outstanding.

Stuffing

2 tablespoons butter
1 (10 1/2-ounce) can minced clams, drained
1/2 cup cooked rice
1/4 cup seasoned bread crumbs
1 tablespoon minced fresh parsley
1 tablespoon minced onion
1 tablespoon lemon juice
1 clove garlic, minced

Fish

1 pound flounder fillets, at least 1/2-inch thick, or any firm
   white fish
2 tablespoons butter
1/4 cup white wine
Chopped fresh parsley
Lemon wedges

Melt butter in nonstick pan. Add clams, rice, bread crumbs, parsley, onion, lemon juice, and garlic. Toss lightly over low heat for 1 minute or until well blended.

Spread 2 tablespoons of clam-rice filling on top of each flounder fillet. Roll up jelly-roll fashion, starting with widest end of the fillet. Place flounder rolls, seam side down, in a single layer in steamer pan. Dot each roll with butter; pour white wine over all. Steam until fish is opaque and flakes easily, 20 to 25 minutes.

Remove carefully to heated serving platter; pour some liquid from steamer dish over the top. Garnish with fresh parsley and lemon wedges. Serve immediately.

Serves 4

Variations

- Vary stuffing with ingredients on hand.
- Mix together 1 1/2 cups cooked rice with 2 cups drained and chopped canned tomatoes, 1/2 cup minced onion, 1/2 teaspoon curry powder, salt, and freshly ground black pepper to taste. Proceed to fill and steam as directed.

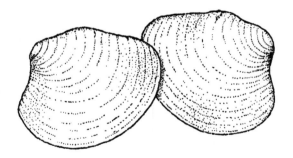

African Fish Stew

West Africans serve corn, rice, plantains, and yams with their stews. They are the mainstay of their diet. The amount of sauce, stew, or soup accompanying the starch depends on the family's resources.

1 red bell pepper, cored, seeded, and sliced
1/2 teaspoon salt
1 teaspoon cayenne pepper
1/2 cup lemon juice
2 tablespoons vinegar
1 tablespoon peanut oil
1 1/2 pounds fish fillets
2 medium onions, sliced
2 tablespoons peanut oil
1 cup water
4 cups hot cooked rice

Combine pepper slices, salt, cayenne pepper, lemon juice, vinegar, and peanut oil. Pour over fish and sliced onions in a bowl. Marinate 6 hours; drain fish and onions, reserving marinade.

When ready to prepare dish, broil fish on oiled pan until golden on both sides. Heat peanut oil in nonstick pan; sauté drained, marinated onions until limp and golden. Add marinade, grilled fish, and 1 cup water to pan. Cover and cook over low heat 10 minutes. Serve over hot rice.

Serves 4

Steamed Ginger Shrimp

Marinate shrimp before steaming for a different taste from an old favorite.

1 pound fresh shrimp, shelled and deveined
1/4 cup oil
1/4 cup soy sauce
1/2 cup sherry
1 clove garlic, minced
1/8 teaspoon grated fresh ginger

To make marinade, mix together oil, soy sauce, sherry, garlic, and ginger until well blended. Pour over shrimp; marinate 1 hour.

Place shrimp (with or without marinade) in steaming pan. Cover and steam shrimp until pink, about 5 minutes.

Serves 2 to 4

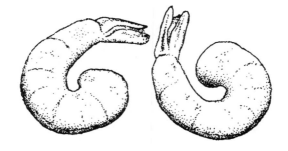

Shrimp with Tomatoes, Onions, and Peppers

Shrimps are simmered in a thick, dry tomato sauce filled with onions and peppers.

2 tablespoons olive oil
2 medium onions, chopped
2 medium peppers, cored, seeded, and chopped
3 fresh tomatoes, cored, seeded, and chopped,
    or 1/2 cup tomato sauce
1 pound fresh shrimp, shelled and deveined, or 1 pound
    cleaned frozen shrimp, thawed and drained
Salt and freshly ground black pepper to taste
4 cups hot cooked rice

Sauté onions and peppers in hot oil in nonstick pan, stirring occasionally, until onions and peppers are slightly brown, about 10 minutes. Add tomatoes or sauce to pan; cook, stirring occasionally, about 15 minutes or until it becomes dry and almost sticks to the pan. Add cleaned shrimp, salt, and pepper. Cook, stirring occasionally, until shrimps turn pink, about 5 minutes. Serve with hot cooked rice.

Serves 4

Stir-Fry Shrimp in Black Bean Sauce

Fresh shrimp should be firm to the touch and have a fresh, slightly sweet odor.

1 pound shrimp, shelled and deveined
3 tablespoons vegetable oil
2 tablespoons fermented black beans, rinsed and crushed
2 cloves garlic, minced
2 tablespoons minced fresh ginger
1/2 teaspoon sugar
2 tablespoons dry sherry
3 scallions with green tops, chopped
4 cups hot rice

Stir-fry shrimp in hot oil in wok or nonstick pan until shrimp turn pink, about 3 minutes. Add black beans, garlic, and ginger; stir-fry 15 seconds. Add sugar and sherry; cook, stirring, until hot, about 15 seconds. Add scallions; toss quickly, about 1 minute. Serve with hot rice.

Serves 4

Shrimp and Eggplant Creole

Absolutely the best!

2 tablespoons olive oil
1 tablespoon minced onion
1 clove garlic, minced
1 cup uncooked rice
2 1/4 cups chicken broth
Dash of Tabasco sauce
2 tablespoons olive oil
2 cups chopped onion
1 cup chopped green pepper
1 cup chopped celery
2 cloves garlic, minced
1 (2-pound, 3-ounce) can plum tomatoes, undrained
1 (8-ounce) can tomato paste
1/2 teaspoon salt
1/4 teaspoon freshly ground black pepper
1 teaspoon Worcestershire sauce
1 bay leaf
1/2 teaspoon thyme
3 slices lemon peel
2 whole cloves
Pinch of sugar
3 tablespoons olive oil
1 medium eggplant, diced, with skin left on
1 1/2 pounds fresh shrimp, shelled and
    deveined with tails left on
2 tablespoons minced fresh parsley
1 tablespoon capers

Sauté onion and garlic in olive oil in nonstick pan until limp. Combine rice, broth, and Tabasco sauce with onion mixture in steaming pan. Cover and steam until rice is done, about 20 minutes.

Sauté onion, green pepper, and celery in oil in heavy pot until vegetables are lightly browned, about 5 minutes. Add garlic, tomatoes, tomato paste, salt, pepper, Worcestershire sauce, bay leaf, thyme, lemon peel, cloves, and sugar. Simmer 10 minutes.

Meanwhile, sauté eggplant in hot oil in nonstick pan until almost tender. Add sautéed eggplant to tomato mixture; simmer 10 minutes. Add shrimp; simmer until shrimp turn pink, about 5 minutes. Discard lemon peel and bay leaf. Stir in parsley and capers. Serve over hot rice.

Serves 4 to 6

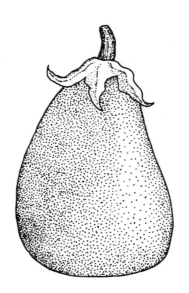

Shrimp and Arugula Risotto

The slightly bitter taste of arugula contrasts nicely with the shrimp.

1 pound shrimp, peeled and deveined
1 bunch arugula, washed, trimmed, and chopped
2 tablespoons olive oil or butter
2 scallions with green tops, minced
2 cloves garlic, minced
1 cup uncooked rice
1/2 cup dry white wine
3 cups chicken broth
Salt and freshly ground black pepper to taste

Sauté shrimp in olive oil in nonstick pan until they begin to turn pink, 2 to 3 minutes. Remove from pan; reserve with prepared arugula.

Sauté scallions and garlic in same pan until limp. Add more oil if necessary. Add rice; stir until translucent, about 2 minutes. Add wine; cook, stirring constantly, until all the liquid is almost absorbed.

Combine rice mixture with broth in steaming pan. Season with salt and pepper to taste. Stir once; cover and steam until rice is done, 16 to 18 minutes. Stir in shrimp and arugula, adding more liquid if too dry. Cover for 3 to 4 minutes. Shrimp should be pink. Rice should be moist. Add more liquid if necessary.

Serves 4

Shrimp Pilaf

A touch of saffron in a tomato-flavored pilaf complements shrimp beautifully.

2 tablespoons oil
1 pound fresh shrimp, shelled and deveined, or uncooked
 frozen shrimp, thawed and drained
1 medium onion, thinly sliced
2 cloves garlic, minced
2 medium tomatoes, peeled, seeded, and chopped
2 stalks celery, sliced
1 teaspoon minced fresh parsley
1/4 teaspoon powdered saffron
1 cup uncooked rice
1 1/2 cups clam juice
Freshly ground black pepper to taste

Sauté shrimp in hot oil in nonstick pan for 1 minute on each side. Remove shrimp; reserve. Add onion and garlic to pan; sauté until onion is limp and golden. Stir in tomatoes, celery, and parsley; cook until blended. Add saffron and rice; cook 2 minutes, stirring constantly.

Combine with clam juice in steaming pan; season with black pepper. Cover and steam rice until done, 18 to 20 minutes. Place shrimp on top; cover for 3 to 4 minutes. Fluff with fork before serving.

Serves 4

Variation

- Cleaned scallops or clams may be substituted for the shrimp.

How to Clean Shellfish

Scrub clams, mussels, and oysters thoroughly with a stiff brush
before steaming. To remove sand and grit, soak in 1 gallon cold
water with 1/3 cup salt. Let stand 15 to 20 minutes to allow clams
or other shellfish to cleanse themselves of sand which will settle
to the bottom of the pan. Change the water and repeat process
several times. Drain clams and rinse thoroughly. Wash clams
thoroughly, discarding any with broken shells.

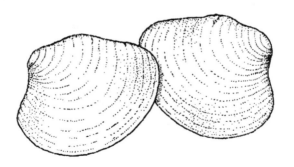

New England Steamed Clams

The hard-shell is called "quahog" in New England, where "clam" generally means the soft-shell variety.

24 cherrystone or littleneck clams, soaked and scrubbed
$1/2$ cup water
Melted butter
Lemon or lime wedges

Place cleaned clams and water in steamer pan. Steam until clams open, about 8 minutes. Discard any that don't open. Serve hot in the shell with melted butter. Pass lemon or lime wedges.

Serves 2 to 4

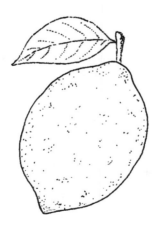

Chinese Steamed Clams

Clams and oysters are very much alike. Preparation and recipes are mostly interchangeable.

24 cherrystone or littleneck clams, soaked and scrubbed
1/2 cup soy sauce
3/4 cup sherry
1 teaspoon minced fresh ginger
1 teaspoon sesame oil

Place cleaned clams in steamer pan. Mix together soy sauce, sherry, and ginger. Pour over the top of the clams. Steam until clams open, about 8 minutes. Sprinkle with sesame oil before serving.

Serves 2 to 4

Variation

- Steam clams plain. Serve with a dipping sauce made by mixing together 2 tablespoons minced, fresh red hot peppers, 1/4 cup light soy sauce, and 2 teaspoons sesame oil.

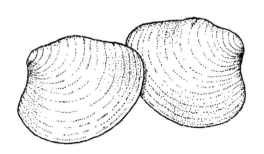

Mussels Marinières

The shell of a mussel is so thin that there is considerably more food in a pound of mussels than in a pound of oysters or clams.

1 pound mussels, soaked and scrubbed
1 tablespoon olive oil
1/3 cup chopped onion
1 1/2 teaspoons flour
1/2 cup dry white wine
Salt and freshly ground black pepper to taste
1 tablespoon chopped fresh parsley

Place cleaned mussels in steaming pan. Cover and steam until the shells open, about 5 minutes. Discard any unopened mussels; reserve juice. Put mussels in serving dish; keep warm.

To make sauce, sauté onion in hot oil until limp and golden. Stir in flour until blended. Stir in reserved juice from mussels and white wine. Simmer, stirring constantly, until thickened, about 3 minutes. Season with salt and black pepper; stir in chopped parsley.

Pour sauce over mussels; serve immediately.

Serves 2 to 4

Turkish Stuffed Mussels

Not as much work as it first appears.

2 onions, finely chopped
1/4 cup olive oil
1 tablespoon pine nuts
1 cup uncooked rice
1 tomato, cored, seeded, and diced
1 tablespoon dried currants
Freshly ground black pepper to taste
1/2 teaspoon allspice
1/2 teaspoon sugar
1 cup beef broth
24 large mussels, soaked and scrubbed
1 lemon, cut in wedges
Chopped fresh parsley

Sauté onion in hot oil in nonstick pan until limp and golden. Add pine nuts and rice; sauté until rice is translucent, about 2 minutes. Stir in tomatoes; simmer 1 minute.

Combine rice mixture with currants, pepper, allspice, sugar, and broth in steaming pan; cover and steam until rice is almost done, 15 to 16 minutes.

Open mussels by running a knife inside the straighter side, saving mussel liquid, straining if necessary. Cut off beard or any hanging threads. Fill shells with rice stuffing; place mussels in baking pan. Bake at 350°F for 20 to 30 minutes.

Serve at room temperature. Decorate with lemon wedges and parsley.

Serves 2 to 4

Italian Seafood Stew

Just about any fish will work.

2 tablespoons olive oil
1 large onion, chopped
2 cups tomato sauce
Freshly ground black pepper to taste
Crushed red pepper to taste
1 pound fresh shrimp, shelled and deveined
1 dozen cherrystone or littleneck clams, soaked and scrubbed
4 cups hot cooked rice
Minced fresh parsley

Sauté onions in hot oil in nonstick pan until limp and golden. Add tomato sauce, black pepper, and crushed red pepper; simmer until sauce thickens, about 10 minutes. Add shrimp and clams; simmer until clams open and shrimp turn pink, 5 to 8 minutes. Serve over hot cooked rice. Sprinkle with parsley.

Serves 4

Variation

• Add 1 tablespoon sliced green or black olives, 1 stalk celery with leaves, chopped, and 1 tablespoon drained capers when tomato is added.

Old-Fashioned Seafood Casserole

Any combination of leftover seafood can be used in this casserole flavored with sherry.

2 tablespoons butter or margarine
1 tablespoon chopped onion
1 tablespoon chopped green pepper
2 tablespoons flour
1 cup milk
$^{1}/_{2}$ cup cream
1 $^{1}/_{2}$ cups cooked rice
1 $^{1}/_{2}$ cups flaked cooked seafood
1 tablespoon minced pimiento
3 tablespoons shredded cheddar cheese
1 tablespoon sherry
Salt and freshly ground black pepper to taste
$^{1}/_{2}$ cup buttered bread crumbs

Sauté onion and green pepper in butter in nonstick pan until onion is limp and golden; push to one side of pan. Blend flour into butter to make a roux; add milk and cream, stirring constantly, until thickened.

Mix rice, fish, pimiento, cheese, sherry, salt, and pepper with sauce. Spoon mixture into a buttered baking dish. Sprinkle with buttered bread crumbs. Bake in 350°F oven for 30 minutes or until brown and bubbly.

Serves 4

CHAPTER 6

Poultry

Chicken and other poultry steam beautifully. The flesh firms up, yet remains juicy, and the texture takes on a silky quality. Removing the skin and visible fat before cooking reduces the calories by approximately half.

Any stuffed fowl can be steamed instead of roasted. The cooking time will be much the same. A whole chicken cooks in about an hour while chunks of chicken cook in about fifteen minutes. Fryers, which can be cut into smaller pieces easily, cook faster than larger chicken pieces unless quartered or halved. Breast meat cooks faster than dark meat and should be removed from the cooker first.

Steam poultry in a dish so cooking juices are not lost in the steaming liquids and can be used as a natural sauce. It also makes a perfect foil for various sauces.

Steamed poultry is particularly good for salads as the flesh is so moist and tender.

Steamed Chicken

A basic recipe with a touch of Asia. Steaming time depends upon the size of the pieces and how crowded the steaming pan is.

1 (2-pound) chicken, skinned and cut into small pieces
2 tablespoons soy sauce
2 tablespoons dry sherry
1 teaspoon minced fresh ginger
2 teaspoons fermented black beans
1 teaspoon brown sugar
1 lemon, thinly sliced

Mix together all ingredients except lemon. Pour over chicken in steaming pan. Place lemon slices on top of the chicken. Steam until tender, 30 to 45 minutes.

Serves 4

Variations

- Delete fresh ginger, black beans, and brown sugar. Add 1 tablespoon olive oil, 1 minced garlic clove, 1 tablespoon minced fresh rosemary or marjoram, and freshly ground black pepper to taste.
- Steam chicken with soy sauce, freshly ground black pepper, and lemon slices.
- Rub chicken pieces with olive oil; season with salt to taste. Steam with lemon slices on top.

Chinese Steamed Chicken with Tangy Sauce

A tangy sauce with a touch of red pepper is served over steamed chicken.

1 (2-pound) chicken, skinned and cut into small pieces
1 tablespoon minced fresh ginger
$1/8$ teaspoon crushed Szechwan peppercorns
Salt to taste

Sauce

2 tablespoons oil
1 teaspoon crushed red pepper
2 tablespoons minced ginger
2 scallions with green tops, minced
2 cloves garlic, minced
1 tablespoon soy sauce
$1/4$ cup vinegar
$1/4$ cup sugar

Place chicken in steaming pan; sprinkle with salt, ginger, and crushed peppercorns. Cover and steam until chicken is tender, 30 to 45 minutes.

When chicken is almost done, heat oil in nonstick pan. Stir-fry red pepper, ginger, scallion, and garlic for 15 seconds. Add soy sauce, vinegar, and sugar. Simmer over low heat until sauce thickens slightly. Pour hot sauce over cooked chicken; serve immediately.

Serves 4

Arroz con Pollo

Chicken and saffron rice is a Spanish dish that has gained tremendous popularity in America.

1 (2-pound) chicken, skinned and cut into small pieces
Salt and freshly ground black pepper to taste
1/4 teaspoon paprika
3 tablespoons oil
1 medium onion, chopped
1 clove garlic, minced
1/2 tablespoon lemon juice
1 cup uncooked rice
1/8 teaspoon saffron
4 cups canned tomatoes, undrained
1 green pepper, cored, seeded, and chopped
1 1/2 cups chicken broth

Sprinkle chicken with salt, pepper, and paprika. Sauté chicken, onion, and garlic in hot oil in nonstick pan until chicken is brown on all sides, turning occasionally. Place chicken-onion mixture in steaming pan. Sprinkle lemon juice, rice, and saffron on chicken. Add tomatoes, green pepper, and broth. Cover and steam until rice is done, about 20 minutes. Add more liquid and adjust seasoning if necessary. Allow to rest 3 to 4 minutes more. Fluff with fork before serving.

Serves 4

Lemon Chicken

The Spanish introduced lemons to this country when they established themselves in St. Augustine, Florida, in 1565. Few fruits add so much zest to foods as lemon does.

2 tablespoons cornstarch
1 tablespoon soy sauce
1 pound boneless chicken breasts, cut in 1-inch pieces
1/2 cup sugar
3/4 teaspoon grated lemon peel
3 tablespoons soy sauce
2 tablespoons lemon juice
2 teaspoons cornstarch
1/4 cup water
1 bunch scallions with green tops, cut in 1-inch pieces
2 tablespoons vegetable oil
4 cups hot cooked rice

Mix 2 tablespoons cornstarch and 1 tablespoon soy sauce with chicken in bowl. Reserve.

Mix together sugar, lemon peel, 3 tablespoons soy sauce, and lemon juice with 2 teaspoons cornstarch and 1/4 cup water. Reserve.

Stir-fry chicken and scallions in wok or nonstick pan until chicken is done, about 3 minutes. Remove chicken-scallion mixture from pan. Reserve.

Add sugar-soy sauce mixture to pan. Bring to boil; cook, stirring until slightly thickened, about 1 minute. Add chicken and scallions; stir to coat all pieces with sauce. Serve with rice.

Serves 4

Country Captain

The name of this dish makes it sounds as if it originated down South, but it comes from India, which explains the touch of curry.

1 (2-pound) chicken, skinned and cut up
1/8 cup flour
2 tablespoons olive oil or butter
1 clove garlic, minced
1 small onion, chopped
1 green pepper, cored, seeded, and chopped
2 cups canned tomatoes, undrained
1 cup chicken broth
1 1/2 tablespoons curry powder
1/2 teaspoon thyme
1/2 teaspoon salt
1/4 teaspoon freshly ground black pepper
1/4 cup raisins or currants
4 cups hot cooked rice
1/4 cup toasted, slivered almonds
1 tablespoon minced fresh parsley

Dust chicken lightly with flour; sauté chicken in hot oil in non-stick pan until lightly browned on all sides, about 15 minutes. Remove chicken from pan. Reserve.

Add garlic, onion, and green pepper to pan; sauté until onion is limp and golden. Return chicken to pan. Add tomatoes, broth, curry, thyme, salt, and pepper; bring to boil. Lower heat; cover and simmer gently 15 minutes. Add raisins; simmer uncovered 15 minutes longer. Serve with rice. Sprinkle with almonds and fresh parsley.

Serves 4

Variation

- Prepare this dish earlier in the day. Add raisins and proceed with the rest of the steps just before you are ready to serve.

Chicken Kebabs

The word *kebab* means "small piece of roasted meat." Kebabs are of Near Eastern origin and are a feature of the cuisines of Turkey, Iran, Iraq, Lebanon, Syria, and India.

2 whole chicken breasts, boned, skinned, and cut in 1 1/2-inch
  chunks
1/3 cup soy sauce
1/3 cup sherry
2 tablespoons sugar
2 tablespoons minced fresh ginger
12 scallions
4 cups hot cooked rice
2 tablespoons butter, at room temperature (optional)

Combine soy sauce, sherry, sugar, and ginger together. Marinate chicken in sauce for 15 minutes. Drain chicken. Thread skewers, alternating chicken and scallions. Broil or steam until chicken is done, about 10 minutes. Toss rice with butter. Serve kebabs on rice.

Serves 4

Variation

- Ten minutes after rice cooker has been turned on, quickly put skewers of chicken in a single layer on top of rice or push down into rice. Cover and finish cooking rice. Allow flavors to blend 3 to 4 minutes more before removing kebabs and fluffing rice with a fork. Serve kebabs on top of rice.

Chicken Polynesian

Ginger, curry, almonds, and coconut are familiar ingredients in Polynesian dishes.

2 whole chicken breasts, skinned and halved
1 cup sour cream
1 clove garlic, minced
Salt to taste
$1/8$ cup flour
2 tablespoons oil
$1/4$ cup water
$1/4$ cup chopped onion
1 tablespoon flour
$1/4$ teaspoon ground ginger
1 clove garlic
$1 1/2$ tablespoons curry powder
4 cups hot cooked rice
2 tablespoons toasted almonds
2 tablespoons shredded coconut

Marinate chicken in sour cream mixed with garlic and salt for 1 hour. Drain chicken, reserving liquid.

Dust chicken with flour. Sauté chicken in hot oil in non-stick pan until browned on all sides. Add water and onion; cover and simmer until chicken is tender, about 10 minutes.

Blend flour with ginger, garlic clove, and curry; mix with reserved sour cream mixture. Add slowly to chicken mixture, stirring constantly, until thickened. Discard garlic clove. Serve with rice. Sprinkle with almonds and coconut.

Serves 4

Variations

- Substitute unflavored yogurt for sour cream; add 1 teaspoon cornstarch to keep it from separating upon heating.
- Another substitute for sour cream is 1 cup lowfat cottage cheese blended with 1 tablespoon lemon juice and 2 tablespoons skim milk.

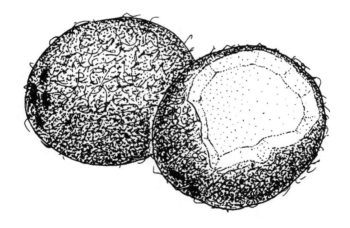

Chicken and Shrimp Gumbo

Gumbo is an American dish born of the meeting of French, Spanish, and African cookery in Old New Orleans kitchens. Gumbo takes its name from a corruption of the African Bantu word for okra, one of its main ingredients.

2 tablespoons olive oil
1 (2-pound) chicken, skinned and cut into small pieces
1/4 cup chopped onion
2 cups sliced fresh okra, or 1 (10-ounce) package frozen,
    thawed and drained
2 cups canned tomatoes, undrained
1 clove garlic, minced
1/4 lemon, thinly sliced
1 bay leaf
3 cups hot water
1/2 teaspoon salt
1/4 teaspoon paprika
1/8 teaspoon Tabasco sauce
1 teaspoon Worcestershire sauce
1/2 pound fresh shrimp, shelled and deveined, or 1/2 pound
    frozen shrimp, thawed and drained
2 tablespoon butter or margarine
2 tablespoons flour
4 to 6 cups hot cooked rice

Sauté chicken and onion in hot oil in nonstick pan until lightly browned. Add okra, tomatoes, garlic, lemon slices, and bay leaf; bring to boil. Add hot water, salt, paprika, Tabasco sauce, and Worcestershire sauce. Lower heat; simmer, partially covered, 30 minutes or until chicken is tender. Add shrimp during last 10 minutes; cook until shrimp turn pink.

Heat butter; blend with flour until smooth; stir into ¹/₂ cup hot broth. Stir mixture slowly into simmering gumbo. Remove bay leaf. Serve with hot cooked rice.

Serves 4 to 6

Variations

- This recipe doubles or triples easily for a large crowd.
- Prepare earlier in the day. Add shrimp just before serving.

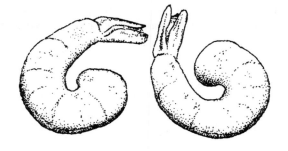

Mandarin Chicken

Chicken with orange sauce is always a favorite.

1 (2-pound) chicken, skinned and cut into small pieces,
    or 1 pound chicken cutlets
1/2 teaspoon salt
1/8 teaspoon freshly ground black pepper
2 tablespoons butter or margarine
1 tablespoon flour
1 (12-ounce) can frozen orange juice, undiluted
2 (11-ounce) cans mandarin oranges, undrained
1 scallion with green top, minced
4 cups hot cooked rice

Season chicken with salt and pepper. Sauté chicken in butter in nonstick pan until brown on all sides. Cover and cook for 20 minutes or until chicken is tender. Remove chicken to serving dish. Keep warm.

Drain off all but 1 tablespoon of juices from pan. Stir flour into pan scrapings; add orange juice, mandarin oranges, and scallion; stir for 2 minutes. Sauce will turn a nice brown color. Serve sauce over chicken with hot rice.

Serves 4

Mexican Chicken Stew

Highly seasoned with onion, green pepper, garlic, and chile powder, this Mexican dish is a fresh, peppery version of classic stewed chicken. Raisins and black olives add an unusual note.

1 (2-pound) chicken, skinned and cut into small pieces
1/8 cup flour
2 tablespoons oil
1 medium onion, sliced
1 small green pepper, cored, seeded, and chopped
2 cloves garlic, minced
4 tablespoons tomato paste
1 1/2 cups water
1 teaspoon chile powder
1/2 teaspoon salt
4 tablespoons raisins
1/2 cup pitted black olives, sliced
4 cups hot cooked rice

Dust chicken with flour; sauté in hot oil in nonstick pan until brown. Remove chicken from pan. Reserve. Sauté onion, green pepper, and garlic in same pan until lightly browned. Add tomato paste, water, chile powder, and salt; simmer 5 minutes.

Return chicken to pan; cover and simmer gently 30 minutes, or until chicken is tender. Stir in raisins and olives; simmer 5 minutes more to blend flavors. Serve with rice.

Serves 4

Chicken Stroganoff

Using chicken breasts in this old favorite cuts the cooking time considerably.

2 whole chicken breasts, boned, skinned, and halved
Salt to taste
2 tablespoons butter or margarine
1 medium onion, diced
1/2 pound fresh mushrooms, cleaned and sliced
1/4 cup sherry
1/2 teaspoon thyme
1 tablespoon flour
2 tablespoons water
1 cup sour cream
1 1/2 teaspoons paprika
4 cups hot cooked rice

Season chicken with salt. Sauté chicken in butter in nonstick pan until brown on all sides. Add onion and mushrooms; sauté until onion is limp and golden. Add sherry and thyme. Reduce heat. Cover and cook for 5 minutes or until chicken is tender.

Blend flour and water together. Add to skillet; cook, stirring constantly, until thickened. Stir in sour cream and paprika; heat gently. Serve with rice.

Serves 4

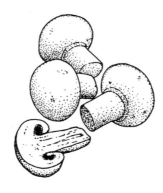

African Chicken and Rice Stew

(*Jollof Rice*)

The best known of the one-dish stews in West Africa is Jollof Rice, common all along the coast.

1 (2-pound) chicken, skinned and cut in small pieces
Salt and freshly ground black pepper to taste
2 tablespoons peanut oil
6 onions, sliced
1/2 tablespoon crushed red pepper
1 (8-ounce) can tomato sauce
3 cups canned tomatoes, undrained
1 cup chicken broth
1 cup water
3 cups hot cooked rice, cooked in chicken broth

Season chicken with salt and pepper. Sauté in hot oil in nonstick pan until brown. Remove chicken from pan. Reserve.

In same pan, sauté onions until limp and golden. Stir in crushed red pepper; sauté briefly. Be careful not to burn. Immediately add tomato sauce, tomatoes, chicken broth, and water. Return chicken to pan; cover and simmer 30 minutes, or until chicken is tender. Adjust seasoning if necessary.

Add cooked rice; allow flavors to blend 3 to 5 minutes, adding more chicken broth or hot water if too thick.

Serves 4

Variation

- Cook rice in stew at end. Add rice with 2 to 3 cups hot water after chicken is tender. Cover and simmer until rice is done.

Chicken and Sausage Risotto

A hearty version of this famous Italian dish.

4 Italian sausages, cut in 1-inch pieces
1 (2-pound) chicken, skinned and cut in small pieces
2 cups canned tomatoes, undrained and crushed
1 cup water
3/4 cup uncooked rice
1 clove garlic, minced
1 medium onion, chopped
1/2 teaspoon salt
1/8 teaspoon freshly ground black pepper
1 bay leaf
1/4 cup freshly grated Parmesan cheese

Sauté sausage in nonstick pan until brown; remove and reserve. Brown chicken in drippings; remove and reserve. Discard fat.

Combine tomatoes, water, rice, garlic, onion, salt, pepper, and bay leaf with sausage and chicken in steaming pan; cover and steam until rice is tender, about 20 minutes. Stir once; add more water if too dry. Sprinkle with grated cheese. Fluff with a fork before serving.

Serves 4

Thai Chicken

Lime juice is an important ingredient in this increasingly popular cuisine.

2 whole chicken breasts, skinned, boned,
and cut in 2-inch strips
2 tablespoons oil
2 tablespoons chopped onion
1/2 cup sliced fresh mushrooms
1 tablespoon minced fresh ginger
1 clove garlic, minced
Pinch of coriander
Salt and freshly ground black pepper to taste
1 1/2 tablespoons soy sauce
1 tablespoon cider vinegar
Juice of 1 lime or lemon
1 teaspoon sugar
4 cups hot cooked rice

Sauté chicken in hot oil in nonstick pan until browned. Add onion, mushrooms, ginger, garlic, coriander, salt, and pepper. Reduce heat; cover and simmer 10 minutes.

Combine soy sauce, vinegar, lime juice, and sugar. Add to chicken; simmer 5 minutes more. Serve with rice.

Serves 4

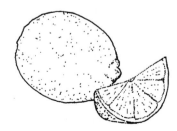

Chicken Tandoor

This authentic recipe comes from Pakistan. Serve with traditional curry accompaniments such as chopped peanuts, yogurt, and chutney.

1 (2-pound) chicken, skinned and quartered
2 large onions, chopped
2 green peppers, cored, seeded, and diced
2 tomatoes, chopped
1/2 teaspoon salt
1 tablespoon curry powder
1 tablespoon coriander
1 tablespoon cumin
1 teaspoon turmeric
1/2 teaspoon cinnamon
1/2 teaspoon garlic powder
1/2 teaspoon freshly ground black pepper, or to taste
2 tablespoons butter, melted (optional)
2 cups water
4 cups hot cooked rice

Suggested Curry Accompaniments

Chopped peanuts
Sieved hard-boiled eggs
Yogurt or sour cream
Grated coconut
Grated onion
Chutney

Place chicken quarters in a single layer in shallow baking dish. Sprinkle with onion, green pepper, tomato, salt, curry powder, coriander, cumin, turmeric, cinnamon, garlic powder, and black pepper. Pour melted butter over the top. Mix with chicken. Cover and marinate in refrigerator several hours if possible.

Add water; bake in 375°F oven for 1 hour, or until chicken is tender. Serve with rice and any of the traditional curry accompaniments.

Serves 4

Variation

• Although traditionally baked, this dish can also be steamed.

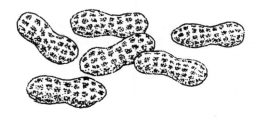

Paella Valenciaga

Paella is always based on rice. In Spain the other ingredients vary according to available food. Chicken and shrimp are coupled with artichokes and green peas in this version.

1 (2-pound) chicken, skinned and cut in small pieces
2 tablespoons olive oil
2 medium tomatoes, cored and cut into eighths
1/2 cup chopped green pepper
1 (10-ounce) package frozen artichokes, thawed and drained
1 small onion, chopped
2 cloves garlic, minced
1 cup uncooked rice
1 teaspoon saffron
3 cups chicken broth
1/2 pound shrimp, shelled and deveined, or 1/2 pound frozen
    shrimp, thawed and drained
1 cup frozen green peas, thawed and drained
1/2 teaspoon salt
1/4 teaspoon paprika

Sauté chicken in hot oil in nonstick pan until chicken is browned. Add tomato, green pepper, artichokes, onion, and garlic to pan; sauté, stirring constantly, until onion is limp, about 5 minutes. Add rice and saffron; stir until rice is translucent, about 2 minutes.

Combine chicken-rice mixture with broth in steaming pan. Cover and steam until rice is almost done, about 15 minutes. Add shrimps, green peas, salt, and paprika. Stir once; cover and steam until rice is done. Shrimp are done when pink. Note: This dish should be dry.

Serves 4

Japanese Chicken and Mushrooms

The Japanese name for this dish—*Oyako Domburi*—means "mother and child." The chicken is served on top of the rice.

1/2 cup chicken broth
1/4 cup soy sauce
1/4 cup sake
1 whole chicken breast, skinned, boned,
    and cut in 1/4-inch strips
4 large fresh mushrooms, sliced
4 scallions with green tops, sliced
4 eggs, beaten
4 cups hot cooked rice

Bring chicken broth, soy sauce, and sake to a boil in pan. Add chicken, mushrooms, and scallions. Reduce heat; simmer gently until chicken and vegetables are done.

Stir in eggs; simmer until eggs are set, stirring gently once. Serve on rice with additional soy sauce.

Serves 4

Greek Chicken Pilaf

A dash of cinnamon and cloves gives an indefinable, delicious, haunting quality to many foods. Serve with sour cream.

2 whole chicken breasts, skinned, boned, and halved
2 tablespoons olive oil or butter
Salt and freshly ground black pepper to taste
1 medium onion, finely chopped
1 cup canned tomatoes, undrained
1 1/2 cups water
Dash of cinnamon
Dash of clove
2/3 cup uncooked rice
1 cup sour cream

Sauté chicken in hot oil in nonstick pan until browned on all sides. Season with salt and black pepper to taste. Add onion, tomatoes, water, cinnamon, and clove; cover and simmer 10 minutes.

Combine chicken-tomato mixture with rice in steaming pan. Cover and steam until rice is done, about 20 minutes. Fluff with fork before serving. Serve with sour cream.

Serves 4

Chicken Livers in White Wine

Fresh mushrooms, onions, and chicken livers are sautéed in butter, then simmered gently in a delicate white wine sauce.

2 tablespoons butter or margarine
1 medium onion, minced
1 cup sliced fresh mushrooms
1 pound chicken livers
2 tablespoons flour
1 cup chicken broth
$^{1}/_{2}$ cup white wine
Salt and freshly ground black pepper to taste
4 cups hot cooked rice

Sauté onion, mushrooms, and chicken livers in butter in nonstick pan until onions are limp and golden. Remove chicken livers and vegetables from pan. Reserve.

Blend flour into pan drippings. Stir in chicken broth, wine, salt, and pepper; cook, stirring constantly, until mixture thickens.

Return chicken livers to pan; simmer 10 minutes, or until done. Serve with rice.

Serves 4

Variation

• Almond rice is especially good with this dish.

Chicken Satay

Fish sauce is a salty condiment made from fermented fish. It is used in Southeast Asia the way soy sauce is used in China and Japan. You can substitute soy sauce, but the flavor won't be authentic. Fish sauce is called *nuoc mam* in Vietnamese and *nam pla* in Thai. It is often referred to by one of these names in Asian markets.

1 teaspoon powdered turmeric
1/2 teaspoon salt
1/2 cup canned unsweetened coconut milk
1 pound chicken breast, skinned, boned,
    and cut in 1-inch by 4-inch strips

Sauce
1 tablespoon minced fresh ginger
1 to 2 serrano or other hot chiles, seeded and minced
1 clove garlic, minced
2 scallions with green tops, minced
1/3 cup creamy peanut butter
1/3 cup canned unsweetened coconut milk,
    chicken broth, or water
2 to 3 tablespoons lime or lemon juice
2 tablespoons fish sauce
1 teaspoon sugar
Chopped fresh cilantro

Combine turmeric, salt, and coconut milk in bowl. Toss chicken strips in mixture to coat. Cover and refrigerate 1 hour.

To make sauce, combine ginger, chiles, garlic, and scallions in bowl. Stir in peanut butter, coconut milk, lime juice, fish sauce, and sugar. Adjust seasoning if necessary: sauce should be sweet and salty. Sprinkle with cilantro. Makes 1 cup.

Drain chicken; thread onto skewers. (Wooden skewers should be soaked in cold water before using.) Steam or broil until just cooked, no more than 1 to 2 minutes on each side. Serve with rice and bowl of peanut sauce on side.

Serves 4

CHAPTER 7

Meats

Meat dishes do not dry out in the rice cooker as they do when cooked by other methods. Seasonings permeate better and the final result offers full-bodied flavor and a delicate texture.

Cheaper cuts of beef such as chuck and brisket give better steaming results than more expensive top round or filet mignon. Likewise, lamb stew and lamb shanks steam more successfully than leg of lamb. However, pork tends to become tough when oversteamed and is sufficiently done when the center has the barest tinge of pink.

Instead of steaming meats on a rack, use a steamer pan so juices will collect and flavorings will not be lost. Serve the juices in place of a high-calorie sauce.

If you marinate meat for a few hours or overnight first, it will be more tender and have more flavor. Seasonings—fresh herbs, garlic, onion—stay moist, and flavors continue to permeate the meat during cooking.

Marinate meats as you would for barbecuing, then steam instead. Steaming time is similar to baking time, but varies due to such factors as size. The only marinades that should not be used are those made with yogurt or other milk products, as they may curdle.

Steamed Beef Rolls

Fillets of beef sold for Italian braciola are lovely stuffed with sautéed mushrooms and cooked on top of steaming rice. To sauté or not to sauté beef briefly is up to you.

4 slices of beef (1/4 inch thick by 3 inches wide),
    pounded until thin
1 tablespoon olive oil (optional)
Salt and freshly ground black pepper to taste

Filling

2 tablespoons butter or margarine
1 medium onion, finely chopped
1/2 pound fresh mushrooms, finely chopped
Salt and freshly ground black pepper to taste
Lemon juice to taste
1/4 cup minced fresh parsley

Sauté beef fillets in oil in nonstick pan on both sides, about 2 minutes. (Or omit step and sauté when stuffed, or steam without sautéing beef. Adjust steaming time.) Season with salt and pepper. Remove from pan. Cool.

To make filling, sauté onions in butter in same pan, adding more butter if necessary. Add mushrooms; season with salt and pepper. Sprinkle with lemon juice; stir until moisture is gone. Stir in parsley. Cool.

Spread mushroom mixture on top of beef fillets. Roll up. Steam separately or place, seam side down, on top of rice in steaming pan 10 minutes after rice cooker has been turned on. Remove and serve as soon as rice is done.

Serves 2 to 4

Beef and Broccoli Stir-Fry

Broccoli has been a favorite vegetable for two thousand years in Greece and Italy. Italian families brought broccoli seed to America and grew broccoli in the suburbs of New York and Boston. Around 1920, commercial growers began producing this prized vegetable.

3/4 pound beef steak, cut in 2-inch strips
1 tablespoon cornstarch
1 tablespoon soy sauce
1 tablespoon dry sherry
1 teaspoon minced fresh ginger
1 clove garlic, minced
1 bunch fresh broccoli (about 1 pound),
    cleaned and cut in pieces
1/4 cup soy sauce
2 tablespoons cornstarch
1 cup water
2 tablespoons oil
1 medium onion, chopped
4 cups hot cooked rice

Mix beef, cornstarch, soy sauce, sherry, ginger, and garlic together in bowl. Marinate 15 minutes. Prepare broccoli by removing florets; cut in half lengthwise. Peel stalks; cut crosswise into 1/4-inch slices. Reserve.

Blend together soy sauce, cornstarch, and water. Reserve. Stir-fry beef in hot oil in wok or nonstick pan 1 to 2 minutes. Remove beef from pan. Reserve.

Heat additional oil in same pan if necessary. Add broccoli and onion; stir-fry 3 to 4 minutes until tender. Add beef and reserved soy sauce mixture. Cook, stirring constantly, until mixture thickens. Serve with rice.

Serves 4

Rice and Meatballs

Spaghetti and meatball lovers will be delighted with this varia-
tion of their favorite dish. Fry, bake, or steam tiny meatballs the
size of large marbles. Add to your favorite tomato sauce and
serve over rice for a delicious meal.

Sauce

2 tablespoons olive oil
2 cloves garlic, halved
1 (2-pound, 3-ounce) can Italian plum tomatoes, undrained
2 tablespoons minced fresh basil, or 1/2 teaspoon dry
1/2 teaspoon salt
1/8 teaspoon freshly ground black pepper
Crushed red pepper

Meatballs

1 pound ground beef or turkey
2 slices dry white bread, grated
2 tablespoons freshly grated Romano cheese
2 cloves garlic, minced
1 tablespoon minced fresh parsley
1/8 teaspoon freshly ground black pepper
2 medium eggs, or 1 egg plus 2 egg whites
6 cups hot cooked rice
1/4 cup freshly grated Parmesan cheese

To make sauce, sauté garlic in hot olive oil in sauce pot until
limp. Strain tomatoes through food mill into pot or blend tomatoes in blender before adding to pot. Add basil, salt, black pepper, and crushed red pepper. Add fried meatballs; simmer 1 hour.

To make meatballs, mix together beef, bread crumbs,
grated cheese, garlic, parsley, and black pepper in bowl. Add
eggs one at a time. Mixture should not be too loose or meatballs will fall apart when fried, baked, or steamed. Wet hands
in cold water before forming meat mixture into tiny balls, the
size of large marbles. Handle meat mixture gently. Do not
pack meatballs.

To fry, heat at least ¹/₄ inch of oil in large skillet. Fry meatballs until crisp and brown on all sides; drain on absorbent paper.
Do not crowd meatballs in skillet. Add meatballs to sauce; simmer sauce slowly 1 hour.

Put hot rice in shallow serving dish. Ladle just enough
sauce on top to coat rice lightly. Sprinkle with cheese, toss, and
serve. Meatballs can be mixed with rice or served separately. Pass
extra cheese and sauce.

Serves 4 to 6

Variations

- Instead of frying meatballs, place in a single layer on baking
  sheet and bake in a 350°F oven until brown. Drain on absorbent paper.
- Serve fried, baked, or steamed meatballs without sauce on favorite rice.
- Serve favorite marinara sauce over rice.

Chili con Carne with Rice

Rice stretches this timeless favorite even further.

2 tablespoons olive oil
1 pound ground beef or turkey
1 small onion, chopped
1 clove garlic, minced
2 (8-ounce) cans tomato sauce
1 cup water
1 tablespoon minced fresh parsley
1 tablespoon minced fresh basil
$1/2$ teaspoon salt
$1/8$ teaspoon freshly ground black pepper
Crushed red pepper to taste
1 (15-ounce) can red kidney beans, washed and drained
6 cups hot cooked rice
$1/2$ cup freshly grated Parmesan cheese

Sauté meat, onion, and garlic in hot oil in nonstick pan until browned. Add tomato sauce, water, parsley, basil, salt, black pepper, and red pepper. Simmer 10 minutes. Add beans; simmer 10 minutes. Adjust seasoning if necessary. Serve with rice. Sprinkle with grated cheese.

Serves 4 to 6

Picadillo

A Spanish mishmash of meat and raisins, usually served with rice and beans.

2 tablespoons olive oil
1 medium onion, finely chopped
1 clove garlic, minced
1 pound ground beef or turkey
2 cups canned tomatoes, undrained and chopped
2 tablespoons raisins
1 teaspoon hot chile pepper
1 teaspoon vinegar
Salt and freshly ground black pepper to taste
4 cups hot cooked rice
3 cups hot cooked black beans, red kidney beans, chick-peas,
   or pink Mexican beans, seasoned with olive oil and garlic
   if desired
1 hard-boiled egg, chopped
Toasted slivered almonds

Sauté meat, onion, and garlic in oil in nonstick pan until browned. Add tomatoes, raisins, chile pepper, vinegar, salt, and pepper. Simmer 30 minutes. Adjust seasoning if necessary. Stew will be rather dry.

Serve with hot rice and beans. Sprinkle with chopped hard-boiled egg and almonds.

Serves 4 to 6

Lamb Shish Kebabs

A Near Eastern dish of meat, usually lamb, broiled on skewers. The name *shish kebab* comes from the Turkish, *shish* meaning "skewer," *kebab* meaning "roast meat."

1 pound boneless lamb, cut in ¹/₂-inch cubes
Lemon juice
Salt and freshly ground black pepper to taste
Dash of oregano
4 cups hot cooked rice or pilaf

Cut 1 pound boneless lamb into ¹/₂-inch cubes. Dip in lemon juice and push onto skewers. Season with salt, pepper, and oregano. Cook under broiler, turning occasionally, until browned on all sides, or steam separately or place on steaming rice to cook. Serve with hot cooked rice or pilaf.

Variation

- Marinate lamb in olive oil, lemon juice, minced fresh parsley, salt, and pepper instead.

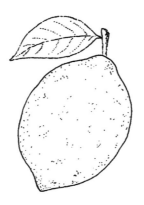

Stuffed Lamb Rolls

The secret is to not overcook these lamb rolls stuffed with spinach, scallions, and feta cheese.

4 slices of lamb (¼ inch thick by 3 inches wide),
    pounded until thin
2 tablespoons olive oil
1½ tablespoons lemon juice
1 clove garlic, minced
½ teaspoon oregano
Salt and freshly ground black pepper to taste

Filling

2 tablespoons olive oil
3 scallions with green tops, chopped
1 (10-ounce) package frozen spinach, thawed and drained
2 tablespoons chopped fresh parsley
¼ cup fresh bread crumbs
1 egg
¼ teaspoon oregano
⅛ teaspoon freshly ground black pepper
¼ teaspoon dill
2 ounces feta cheese, cubed

Combine olive oil, lemon juice, garlic, oregano, salt, and pepper in bowl. Marinate lamb 15 minutes.

To make filling, sauté scallion until limp; add spinach and parsley. Sauté 2 minutes. Cool. Stir in bread crumbs, egg, oregano, black pepper, and dill.

To make rolls, place lamb fillets flat. Spread spinach mixture on top. Arrange feta cubes over spinach. Fold ends in slightly. Roll up. Tie with string. Place seam side down in steaming pan. Add 1 cup water. Steam 30 minutes or until lamb is done to taste. Serve with rice.

Serves 4

Szechwan Lamb

Szechwan is one of five distinct schools of Chinese cooking, very highly seasoned, usually hot.

1 pound lamb, cut in 2-inch strips
3 tablespoons oil

Marinade

1 egg white
1 tablespoon cornstarch
1 tablespoon sherry

Ginger Mixture

2 teaspoons minced fresh ginger
3 hot peppers, shredded
1 bunch scallions, shredded into 2-inch lengths

Soy-vinegar Mixture

3 tablespoons soy sauce
2 tablespoons vinegar
3 tablespoons sherry
1 clove garlic, minced
$1/4$ teaspoon freshly ground black pepper

Cornstarch Mixture

2 teaspoons cornstarch
1 tablespoon sherry

1 tablespoon sesame seed oil
4 cups hot cooked rice

Beat together egg white, cornstarch, and sherry. Marinate lamb in mixture. Combine ginger, hot peppers, and scallions. Reserve. Combine soy sauce, vinegar, sherry, garlic, and pepper. Reserve. Mix cornstarch and sherry together. Reserve.

Stir-fry lamb in hot oil in wok or nonstick pan for 1 to 2 minutes. Remove lamb from pan. Reserve. Stir-fry ginger mixture in pan 1 to 2 minutes. Add reserved lamb and soy-vinegar mixture to pan. Stir-fry 1 minute or until lamb is done. Stir in cornstarch mixture until sauce thickens slightly. Stir in sesame oil. Serve with rice.

Serves 4

Lamb Pilaf

Pilaf or *pilau* is the Persian or Turkish word that refers to a spiced dish of rice simmered with meat or fish.

1/2 pound boneless leg lamb, cut in 1-inch strips
1 tablespoon olive oil
Salt and freshly ground black pepper to taste
1 cup uncooked rice
2 cups chicken or beef broth
1/4 teaspoon powdered saffron
1/4 cup sliced almonds
1/4 cup sesame seeds

Sauté lamb in hot oil in nonstick pan until lightly browned but still pink, stirring frequently. Season with salt and pepper. Remove lamb from pan. Reserve.

Sauté rice in same pan until translucent. Combine rice with lamb, broth, and saffron in steaming pan. Cover and steam until rice is done, about 20 minutes.

Meanwhile, toast almonds and sesame seeds on baking sheet in preheated 300°F oven until golden brown, stirring frequently. Watch closely to prevent burning. When pilaf is done, stir in almonds and sesame seeds. Fluff gently with a fork before serving.

Serves 4

Variations

- Add 2 cups canned tomatoes, undrained and chopped. Decrease broth to 1 cup.
- Add sliced fresh mushrooms.
- Omit almonds and sesame seeds.

Lamb Curry

Curries are native to India where they are mentioned as early as A.D. 477. All curry powders have a characteristic flavor. Turmeric, fenugreek, cumin, coriander, and cayenne pepper are typical ingredients.

1 pound boneless lamb, cut in $^1/_2$-inch cubes
Salt and freshly ground black pepper to taste
4 tablespoons olive oil
1 cup hot water
2 medium onions, finely chopped
$^1/_4$ cup flour
2 teaspoons curry powder
2 cups hot beef broth
2 teaspoons lemon juice
2 tablespoons shredded coconut
4 cups hot cooked rice

Season lamb with salt and pepper. Sauté lamb cubes in 2 table-spoons of oil in nonstick pan until lightly browned, stirring frequently. Add hot water; simmer, covered, 1 hour.

Sauté onions in remaining oil in separate pan until limp and golden. Stir in flour and curry powder. Gradually add beef broth to onion mixture; simmer, stirring constantly, until thickened. Pour sauce over meat. Simmer, covered, 30 minutes or until meat is very tender.

Add lemon juice and coconut. Adjust seasoning if necessary. Arrange border of rice on platter; fill center with curried lamb.

Serves 4

Indonesian Pork

From a culinary point of view, Indonesia is probably the leading country of Southeast Asia having a cuisine that ranks with the other great ones of Asia—Chinese, Japanese, and Indian—in variety and distinction.

2 tablespoons oil
1 pound boneless pork, cut in $1/2$-inch cubes
1 large onion, finely chopped
2 cloves garlic, minced
$1/4$ teaspoon ground chile pepper
$1/3$ cup soy sauce
2 teaspoons brown sugar
1 teaspoon lemon juice
4 cups hot cooked rice

Sauté pork, onions, garlic, and chile pepper in hot oil in nonstick pan for 10 minutes, stirring frequently. Add soy sauce, sugar, and lemon juice. Cook over low heat 10 minutes. Adjust seasoning if necessary. Serve with rice.

Serves 4

Pork Chop Suey

The only difference between chop suey and chow mein is that chow mein is usually served over crisp Chinese noodles. Both are inventions of Chinese-Americans in San Francisco in the nineteenth century.

3 tablespoons oil
2 cups Chinese cabbage, thinly sliced
3 cups celery, thinly sliced
2 cups fresh bean sprouts, cleaned, or 1 (16-ounce) can,
    washed and drained
1 (8-ounce) can sliced water chestnuts
2 teaspoons sugar
Salt and freshly ground black pepper to taste
2 cups chicken broth
2 1/2 tablespoons cornstarch
1/4 cup water
1/4 cup soy sauce
2 cups slivered cooked pork
4 cups hot cooked rice

Prepare all ingredients before beginning to cook. Stir-fry Chinese cabbage, celery, bean sprouts, water chestnuts sprinkled with sugar, salt, and pepper in hot oil in wok or non-stick pan for 2 minutes. Add chicken broth. Cook, stirring occasionally, about 10 minutes.

Mix cornstarch, water, and soy sauce together. Stir into vegetable mixture until it thickens. Add meat; heat thoroughly. Serve over rice.

Serves 4

Rice Lasagna

Everybody's favorite is made with rice instead of pasta. This dish of rice baked with tomato sauce, mozzarella, and grated Parmesan cheese can be made earlier in the day and popped into the oven shortly before guests arrive.

Sauce

1 pound Italian hot and/or sweet sausage, parboiled and cut in
   $1/2$-inch pieces
1 clove garlic, halved
1 (2-pound, 3-ounce) can Italian plum tomatoes, undrained
2 tablespoons minced fresh basil, or $1/2$ teaspoon dried
$1/4$ teaspoon fennel seeds
$1/2$ teaspoon salt
Freshly ground black pepper to taste
1 pound ricotta cheese
3 tablespoons freshly grated Parmesan cheese
2 eggs, beaten
9 cups hot cooked rice
1 pound mozzarella, thinly sliced, or grated
$1/2$ cup freshly grated Romano cheese

Parboil and fry sausage until brown. Remove from pan. Reserve. Pour off all but 1 tablespoon of fat from sauce pot; sauté garlic until limp. Strain tomatoes through food mill into pot or blend tomatoes in blender before adding to pot.

Add basil, fennel seeds, salt, black pepper, and reserved sausage. Simmer slowly, $1 1/2$ hours.

Mix together ricotta, grated Parmesan, and eggs until smooth. Reserve.

To put lasagna together, place a little sauce on bottom of a large shallow baking pan. Spread 3 cups of rice on bottom of pan; top with $1/3$ of both the tomato sauce and ricotta mixture; sprinkle with grated Romano and mozzarella. Arrange as many layers as dish will hold, topping with cheese. Dish can be stretched by using more rice and sauce.

Bake at 400°F for 30 minutes or until hot and bubbly. Allow to rest 10 minutes before serving. Cut in 3-inch by 3-inch squares. Serve with grated Romano cheese and crushed red pepper.

Serves 4 to 6

Variations

- Substitute 32-ounce jar tomato sauce. Add sausage if desired.
- Make lasagna with favorite meatless or vegetable sauce.

Arroz con Platanos

Latin American countries combine sausage and bananas with rice.

1 pound link sausage, cut in 3/4-inch slices
1/2 cup seedless raisins, soaked
3 bananas, cut in 3/4-inch slices
4 cups hot cooked rice
Salt and freshly ground black pepper to taste

Sauté sausage in nonstick pan until well done. Add raisins and bananas; stir gently until well coated, about 3 minutes. Add cooked rice to skillet; toss gently until heated. Season with salt and pepper to taste. Serve immediately.

Serves 4

Variation

- Delete raisins. Sauté sausage or cubed pork with minced garlic clove and small onion. Add bananas and cooked rice. Season with 1/4 cup freshly grated Parmesan cheese. Top with 1/4 cup pitted green olives and 1 sliced hard-boiled egg.

Chinese Sausages and Rice

This is one of the simplest Chinese meals you can make. Available in Chinese or Asian groceries, Chinese sausages are well seasoned with soy sauce, Chinese spices, and alcohol. There are two major types of Chinese sausages. Both are made with pork; one is all pork, the other is pork and duck livers.

2 cups uncooked rice
3 cups water
1 pound (8 or 9 links) Chinese sausage
2 tablespoons soy sauce

Put rice and water in steaming pan; cover and steam 10 minutes. Bury whole sausage links in the rice. Quickly re-cover and continue steaming until rice is done.

Mix cooked rice with soy sauce. Toss rice gently with fork. To serve, slice sausages diagonally into 1/4-inch slices.

Serves 4

Variation

- Meat or poultry that has been marinated for stir-fry can be cooked on top of steaming rice. Add ten minutes after rice cooker has been turned on.

Jambalaya

Jambalaya (derived from the Spanish word *jamon* meaning "ham") was introduced to New Orleans by the Spanish in the late 1700s. It is considered one of the classic Creole dishes.

¹/₄ cup diced salt pork, or 2 slices bacon, diced,
    or 2 tablespoons olive oil
1 medium green pepper, cored, seeded, and diced
1 medium onion, chopped
1 clove garlic, minced
1 ¹/₂ cups diced cooked ham
³/₄ cup uncooked rice
2 ¹/₂ cups canned tomatoes, undrained and chopped
1 cup water
1 tablespoon minced fresh parsley
¹/₂ teaspoon thyme
¹/₂ teaspoon salt
¹/₈ teaspoon freshly ground black pepper
Cayenne pepper to taste
¹/₂ pound fresh shrimp, shelled and deveined, or ¹/₂ pound
    frozen shrimp, thawed and drained
1 cup hot water or chicken broth

If using salt pork or bacon, fry until brown and crisp in nonstick pan. Otherwise, heat oil; add green pepper, onion, and garlic; sauté until lightly browned.

Combine green pepper–onion mixture with ham, rice, tomatoes, water, parsley, thyme, salt, black pepper, and cayenne pepper in steaming pan. Cover and steam until rice is almost done, about 20 minutes.

Five minutes before rice is done, add shrimp to pan. Stir once; cover and steam until rice is done. Shrimp are done when pink. Dish should be moist. Stir in 1 cup hot water or broth before serving if necessary.

Serves 4

Scalloped Ham and Rice Bake

No one knows for sure just when salt was first used to cure ham, but cured ham was traditional at pagan spring festivals which predate the Christian Easter.

2 tablespoons butter or margarine
2 tablespoons flour
2 cups light cream or evaporated milk
2 cups diced cooked ham
2 hard-boiled eggs, chopped
Salt and freshly ground black pepper to taste
1 teaspoon Worcestershire sauce
4 cups hot cooked rice
1 cup bread crumbs
2 tablespoons freshly grated Parmesan cheese
Dots of butter or margarine (optional)

Stir flour into melted butter to make a roux. Slowly add cream, stirring constantly, until thickened. Stir in ham, eggs, salt, pepper, and Worcestershire sauce.

Mix rice with ham sauce; pour into shallow casserole. Top with bread crumbs and cheese. Dot with butter. Bake at 375°F for 15 to 20 minutes until brown and bubbly.

Serves 4

Ham, Asparagus, and Rice Soufflé

Nobody will guess you are using leftovers in this delicious soufflé.

1/2 cup diced cooked asparagus
3 tablespoons butter
1/4 cup flour
1 cup warm milk
1/4 cup sharp cheddar cheese, grated
1/2 teaspoon salt
1 teaspoon dry mustard
4 egg yolks, beaten
4 egg whites, beaten until stiff but not dry
1/2 cup cooked rice
1/4 cup ground cooked ham

Place asparagus in bottom of an ungreased 1 1/2-quart, straight-sided, round soufflé dish. Set aside.

Melt butter in top of double boiler; stir in flour until smooth. Add heated milk a little at a time. Cook, stirring constantly, over boiling water until smooth and thick. Add cheese, salt, and dry mustard; stir until smooth and creamy. Remove from heat.

Stir a little cheese sauce into beaten egg yolks; slowly stir this mixture into rest of cheese sauce.

Beat egg whites until stiff. Fold egg whites, rice, and ham into cheese sauce; pour into soufflé dish. Mixture should not reach top of the dish. To form crown, make a shallow path with the edge of a knife about 1 inch from the edge of the rim all the way around.

Preheat oven to 400°F; bake uncovered for 5 minutes. Lower heat to 375°F; continue baking for 30 minutes, or until golden brown. Serve immediately.

Serves 4

CHAPTER 8

Rice Salads

Rice salads have acquired newfound glamour. Once lowly sustenance for people who had little else, rice salads are now being featured on pricey menus. It's understandable. When properly prepared, rice salads are lush in texture and able to soak up flavor.

Rice salads should not be made earlier than the morning of a dinner party because they lose their flavor if they are left sitting for hours in a refrigerator. They tend to need reseasoning after they have sat for awhile, so taste before serving and adjust seasoning if necessary. Serve at room temperature, not ice-cold, so you can taste the full flavor of the ingredients.

Produce should be impeccably fresh. Although ingredients can be prepared ahead of time for assembling later, certain foods such as seafood are best cooked within a few hours of being served. Vegetables should never be left sitting in the refrigerator. This is particularly important with tomatoes. Add just before serving.

There are no hard and fast rules for making rice salads. Experiment with your own versions. Here are some recipes to get you started.

Wild Rice Salad

Add chopped fresh herbs to wild rice salad just before serving so colors will be at their brightest and most appealing.

1 cup wild rice
1 1/2 cups chicken broth
1 cup water
2 bay leaves
1/4 cup red onion, thinly sliced
1 clove garlic, minced
1/4 cup orange juice
Juice of 1 lemon
1/2 cup olive oil
Salt and freshly ground black pepper to taste
1/2 cup chopped fresh parsley
2 tablespoons fresh basil
2 tablespoons fresh mint
2 tomatoes, cored, seeded, and coarsely chopped

Combine wild rice, chicken broth, water, and bay leaves in steaming pan. Cover and steam until just tender, about 35 minutes. Add more water if rice needs to cook longer. Discard bay leaves. Put rice in serving dish.

   While rice is still warm, add red onion, garlic, orange juice, lemon juice, and half of olive oil; toss gently to coat with juice and oil. Slowly add remaining oil; season with salt and pepper to taste. Just before serving, add freshly chopped herbs and tomatoes.

Serves 4

Variation

• To extend wild rice, mix with an equal amount of cooked brown rice or bulgur wheat.

Almond Rice Salad

Chopped prunes and nuts add an unusual note to this salad.

1/2 cup pitted prunes
Strong tea
3 cups cooked rice
2 small canned red peppers, diced
1/4 cup toasted slivered almonds
1 tablespoon minced fresh parsley
2 tablespoons olive oil
2 tablespoons vinegar
Salt and freshly ground black pepper to taste

Put prunes in bowl; cover with strong tea. Soak 1 hour. Drain and dice.

Mix rice with prunes, peppers, almonds, and parsley in bowl. Blend together olive oil and vinegar; season with salt and pepper to taste. Pour over salad; toss gently.

Serves 4

Peas and Rice Salad

Dill and mustard add zest to the dressing.

2 cups hot cooked rice
1 cup cooked peas
1 cup prosciutto, shredded
1 tablespoon chopped fresh dill

Dressing

1 scallion with green top, minced
1 teaspoon Dijon mustard
1 tablespoon red wine vinegar
2 tablespoons olive oil
1 tablespoon water
1 tablespoon chopped fresh dill
Salt and freshly ground black pepper to taste

To make salad, mix rice with peas, prosciutto, and fresh dill in bowl.

To make dressing, mix together scallion, mustard, vinegar, olive oil, water, and dill; season with salt and pepper to taste. Pour over salad; toss gently. Adjust seasoning if necessary. Serve sprinkled with additional fresh dill.

Serves 4

Curried Peas and Rice Salad

Nuts, raisins, and curry powder make this salad reminiscent of the food of India.

¹/₂ cup raisins
1 cup warm water
3 cups cooked rice
1 cup hazelnuts
1 cup cooked peas
1 tablespoon curry powder
1 cup yogurt
¹/₃ cup mayonnaise
Lemon juice to taste
Salt to taste

Soak raisins 1 hour in warm water. Toss rice with drained raisins, hazelnuts, peas, and curry powder in bowl. Blend yogurt and mayonnaise with lemon juice. Mix with salad ingredients. Season with salt to taste.

Serves 4

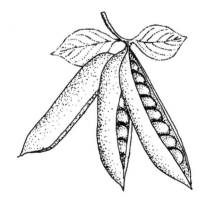

Chick-pea and Rice Salad

Sesame seeds were brought to America by African slaves who called them *benne* or *bene* seed. Here, toasted sesame seeds add an unexpected crunch.

2 cups cooked rice
1 cup canned chick-peas, rinsed and drained
1 red, green, or yellow bell pepper, cored, seeded, and cut in
   $^1/_2$-inch squares
3 scallions with green tops, sliced

Dressing
1 teaspoon sesame oil
$^1/_4$ teaspoon ground cumin
2 tablespoons lemon juice
1 tablespoon olive oil
2 teaspoons toasted sesame seeds
Salt to taste

To make salad, mix rice with chick-peas, pepper, and scallions in bowl.

To make dressing, mix together sesame oil, cumin, lemon juice, olive oil, and sesame seeds; season with salt to taste. Pour over salad; toss gently. Adjust seasoning if necessary.

Serves 4

Lentils and Rice Salad

The lentil is a native of Southwestern Asia. This salad makes a satisfying protein meal mixed with pungent, rather bitter greens.

2 cups hot cooked rice
2 cups cooked lentils

Dressing
1/2 cup minced fresh parsley
1 cup chopped arugula, chicory, or watercress
2 scallions with green tops, minced
3 tablespoons olive oil
1 tablespoon red wine vinegar
Salt and freshly ground black pepper to taste

To make salad, mix rice and lentils together in bowl.

To make dressing, mix together parsley, arugula, scallions, olive oil, and vinegar; season with salt and pepper to taste. Pour over salad; toss gently. Adjust seasoning if necessary.

Serves 4

Hot Italian Rice Salad

Flavors blend delicately in a hot rice salad. Hot vegetable and rice salads tossed with olive oil and lemon or vinegar are favorites in Italy.

3 cups hot cooked rice
1/2 cup chopped celery
1/2 cup chopped green pepper
1 canned pimiento, chopped
2 tablespoons minced fresh parsley
1 cup cooked peas
1/4 cup sliced stuffed green olives
1/4 cup sliced black olives
1/4 cup freshly grated Parmesan cheese
1/2 cup olive oil
Juice of 1 lemon
Freshly ground black pepper to taste

Mix rice with celery, green pepper, pimiento, parsley, peas, olives, and cheese in bowl. Blend together olive oil and lemon juice; season with salt and pepper to taste. Pour over salad; toss gently.

Serves 4

Mediterranean Rice Salad

Tomatoes, black olives, and feta cheese flavored with lemon and fresh basil makes this a memorable rice salad.

1 tomato, cored, seeded, and chopped
1/2 cup oil-cured black olives, pitted and coarsely chopped
1/2 cup crumbled feta cheese
2 stalks celery with leaves, chopped
1 tablespoon chopped fresh parsley
2 cups hot cooked rice

Dressing

1/4 cup fresh lemon juice
2 1/2 tablespoons olive oil
2 cloves garlic, minced
2 teaspoons minced fresh basil or thyme
Salt and freshly ground black pepper to taste

To make salad, combine tomato, olives, feta, celery, and parsley with rice in bowl; toss gently.

To make dressing, mix together lemon juice, olive oil, garlic, and basil or thyme; season with salt and pepper to taste. Pour over salad; toss gently. Adjust seasoning if necessary. Garnish with chopped parsley.

Serves 4

Athenian Salad

A pretty, colorful salad of ham, peaches, and rice.

2 tablespoons butter or margarine
1 cup chopped ham
$^1/_2$ cup chopped green pepper
2 cups canned peach slices, drained
1 teaspoon lemon juice
$^1/_2$ cup green olives
2 cups cooked rice
Salt and freshly ground black pepper
Crisp chilled lettuce

Sauté ham and peppers in melted butter in nonstick pan, 5 minutes or until peppers are lightly brown. Remove from heat. Add peaches, lemon juice, olives, and cooked rice. Season with salt and pepper to taste; toss gently. Allow mixture to blend flavors for 10 to 15 minutes before serving. Serve on lettuce.

Serves 4

Tuna, Vegetable, and Rice Salad

Americans are only now discovering the joys of rice salads containing ever popular tuna fish.

3 cups cooked rice
1 cup chopped celery
1 cup artichoke hearts in oil, sliced
1 cup mushrooms in oil, sliced
1 (7³/₄-ounce can) tuna, drained and flaked
2 medium tomatoes, cored, seeded, and diced
¹/₂ cup black pitted olives, sliced
3 anchovies, chopped
¹/₂ teaspoon capers
1 small red onion, thinly sliced
3 tablespoons olive oil
Salt and freshly ground black pepper to taste

Suggested Garnishes

Lemon wedges
Hard-boiled eggs, quartered
Tomato wedges
Onion rings
Parsley

Toss rice with celery, artichokes, mushrooms, tuna fish, tomatoes, olives, anchovies, capers, onion, and olive oil. Season with salt and black pepper to taste. Garnish with lemon wedges, hard-boiled eggs, tomato wedges, onion rings, and parsley if desired.

Serves 4

Shrimp, Fennel, and Rice Salad

Fennel is an aromatic plant belonging to the carrot family. It is native to the Mediterranean.

2 cups hot cooked rice
1 pound cooked shrimp, shelled and deveined
1 cup slivered fennel
2 tablespoons chopped fresh scallion

Dressing
1 1/2 tablespoons red wine vinegar
1 1/2 tablespoons olive oil
2 tablespoons chopped fresh tarragon
Salt and freshly ground black pepper to taste

To make salad, mix rice with shrimp, fennel, and 1 tablespoon scallion in bowl.

To make dressing, mix together vinegar, olive oil, and tarragon; season with salt and pepper to taste. Pour over shrimp-rice salad; toss gently. Adjust seasoning if necessary. Garnish with scallions.

Serves 4

Ginger Shrimp and Rice Salad

Ginger and toasted sesame seeds add that little extra something to a popular salad.

3 scallions with green tops, finely chopped
1 bunch chives, finely chopped
3 cups cooked rice
2 cups cooked shrimp
$1/2$ cup yogurt
$1/2$ cup mayonnaise
Pinch of ginger
Salt to taste
Lemon juice to taste
Crisp chilled lettuce
Toasted sesame seeds

Mix together scallions, chives, rice, and shrimp in bowl. Blend yogurt and mayonnaise with ginger, salt, and lemon juice to taste. Mix with shrimp mixture. Chill. Serve on lettuce sprinkled with toasted sesame seeds.

Serves 4

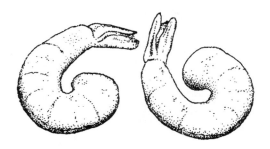

Crabmeat and Rice Salad

Curry powder adds a special spark to seafood salads.

1 medium green pepper, cored, seeded, and chopped
3 pimientos, chopped
2 cups cooked crabmeat, picked over and flaked
2 cups cooked rice
$1/2$ cup yogurt
$1/2$ cup mayonnaise
$3/4$ teaspoon curry powder
Salt to taste
Lemon juice to taste
Crisp chilled lettuce
Minced chives

Mix together green peppers, pimientos, crabmeat, and rice in bowl. Blend yogurt and mayonnaise with curry powder, salt, and lemon juice to taste. Mix with crabmeat mixture. Chill. Serve on lettuce garnished with chives.

Serves 4

Tossed Salad with Chicken, Rice, and Avocado

Avocado is a pretty and delicious addition to salads.

6 cups salad greens, washed, drained, and torn into bite-size
   pieces (mixture of spinach, romaine, chicory, Bibb)
2 hard-boiled eggs, shelled and quartered
1 avocado, peeled and cut lengthwise
1 tablespoon lemon juice
2 medium tomatoes, cored and cut into wedges
1 cup sliced cooked chicken
1 cup cooked rice
$1/2$ teaspoon salt (optional)

Dressing

$3/4$ cup yogurt
2 tablespoons mayonnaise
$1/4$ cup chile sauce
1 hard-boiled egg, finely chopped (optional)
8 pitted black olives, sliced
2 teaspoons minced chives
1 teaspoon lemon juice

Sprinkle avocado with lemon juice. Put cleaned salad greens in bowl. Arrange hard-boiled eggs, avocado, tomatoes, chicken, and rice on top; season with salt to taste.

To make dressing, mix together yogurt, mayonnaise, chile sauce, chopped egg, olives, chives, and lemon juice. Chill if possible. Toss with salad.

Serves 4

Variation

• Serve with your favorite oil-and-vinegar dressing instead.

Chicken and Rice Salad

When rice is being made into a salad, it is best to prepare the dressing before the rice has cooked. Toss hot rice immediately with the dressing so flavors can marry as the ingredients cool.

$1/2$ pound boneless chicken breasts, cut in $1/2$-inch cubes

Marinade

3 serrano peppers, stemmed, seeded, and minced
2 cloves garlic, minced
$1/2$ teaspoon grated lime peel
$1/4$ cup lime juice

Salad

2 cups hot cooked rice
1 tablespoon chopped fresh parsley
1 tablespoon chopped fresh cilantro
1 tablespoon chopped fresh mint
2 serrano peppers, stemmed, seeded, and minced

Dressing

1 tablespoon lime juice
1 tablespoon olive oil
Salt and freshly ground black pepper to taste

Garnish

4 lime slices

To make marinade, combine peppers, garlic, lime peel, and lime juice. Add chicken and coat well. Refrigerate 1 hour, then remove chicken breasts from marinade. Steam in steaming pan until done, about 15 minutes.

To make salad, mix rice with parsley, cilantro, mint, and peppers in bowl. Toss with chicken.

To make dressing, mix together lime juice, olive oil, salt, and pepper. Pour over chicken salad; toss gently. Adjust seasoning if necessary. Garnish with lime slices.

Serves 4

Chicken Salad Stuffed Tomatoes

Tomatoes stuffed with chicken, avocado, and rice make a spectacular luncheon dish.

1 large avocado, peeled and diced
1 tablespoon lemon juice
1 cup diced cooked chicken
3/4 cup cooked rice
1/2 cup diced celery
1 teaspoon minced scallion
2 tablespoons yogurt
2 tablespoons sour cream
Salt to taste
4 large ripe tomatoes
Crisp chilled lettuce

Sprinkle avocado with lemon juice. Reserve. Mix together chicken, rice, celery, scallion, yogurt, and sour cream. Season with salt to taste. Add avocado; toss gently.

Cut off tops of tomatoes; scoop out and discard pulp. Fill with chicken-avocado mixture; replace tops. Serve on lettuce.

Serves 4

Molded Chicken, Pineapple, and Rice Salad

Crushed pineapple, diced celery, rice, and pecans give this chicken salad an unusually elegant flair.

1 (3-ounce) package orange-pineapple gelatin
1³/₄ cups hot chicken broth
Dash of black pepper
Dash of paprika
2 tablespoons vinegar
2 tablespoons yogurt
2 tablespoons mayonnaise
1¹/₂ cups diced cooked chicken
³/₄ cup cooked rice
¹/₂ cup minced celery
1 tablespoon minced pimiento
1 tablespoon minced fresh parsley
¹/₄ cup canned crushed pineapple, drained
2 tablespoons coarsely chopped pecans
2 tablespoons sweet pickle relish

Crisp chilled lettuce
Cherry tomatoes
Sour cream or yogurt

Dissolve gelatin in hot chicken broth. Cool slightly. Mix in black pepper, paprika, vinegar, yogurt, and mayonnaise; blend well. Chill until thick but not set. Fold in remaining ingredients. Pour into a 1¹/₂-quart mold. Chill until firm. Unmold on lettuce; surround with cherry tomatoes. Serve with sour cream or yogurt.

Serves 4

CHAPTER 9

Breads and Stuffings

*B*oston Brown Bread is probably the best-known steamed bread in America today. This moist and richly colored bread has been popular in New England since Colonial times. Just about any quick bread recipe that is normally baked can be steamed, but it is best to choose those that have ingredients such as molasses or dark spices to offset the paleness that results from steaming. The top crust does not develop a golden color or the characteristic cracking that results with baking. Most yeast breads that are customarily baked are not good candidates for steaming.

Southern cooks have a long history of adding rice to breads. Probably because of the rich tradition of rice cookery that sprang up after rice became a major crop in South Carolina in the eighteenth century.

The addition of rice to muffins, popovers, waffles, and pancakes adds a nutty texture and chewiness without the calories of nuts. Brown rice is an especially good choice.

No collection of rice breads would be complete without the South's famous Calas, sweet fried rice cakes.

Boston Brown Bread

Here is my recipe for the famous dark brown steamed bread made with cornmeal and sweetened with molasses.

1 cup cornmeal
1 cup whole wheat flour
1 cup white flour
1 teaspoon salt
1 teaspoon baking soda
1 3/4 cups milk
1 cup molasses
1 cup raisins

Sift cornmeal, flour, salt, and baking soda together in bowl. Add milk and molasses; stir until blended. Mix in raisins.

Traditionally, this bread is baked in soup cans, but steamer pans can be used. Grease cans (or pans); fill two-thirds full with batter; cover with lid or aluminum foil. Steam 2 hours. Remove breads from cans.

Makes 5 small loaves

Variation

- Place cans in pan containing at least 1 inch of water. Steam 2 hours in 375°F oven.

Calas

(Fried Rice Cakes)

These delicious little cakes sprinkled with sugar and cinnamon are favorites in New Orleans with morning coffee.

1/2 package dry yeast
1/2 cup warm water
1 1/2 cups hot cooked rice, mashed and cooled to lukewarm
3 eggs, beaten
1 1/4 cups flour, sifted
1/4 cup sugar
1/2 teaspoon salt
1/4 teaspoon nutmeg
Oil for frying
Powdered sugar, or sugar and cinnamon

Dissolve yeast in warm water. Stir in lukewarm rice; mix well. Cover and let rise in warm place overnight. Add eggs, flour, sugar, salt, and nutmeg; beat until smooth. Let rest in warm place 30 minutes.

Heat oil to 375°F. Drop mixture by spoonfuls into hot oil. Fry until golden brown, about 3 minutes. Drain on absorbent paper. Serve hot, sprinkled with powdered sugar or sugar mixed with cinnamon.

Serves 6

Variation

• Calas are also delicious served with warmed fruit or maple syrup.

Rice Muffins

Muffins made without yeast are typical of Native American cookery. Moist and chewy, rice muffins are also quick and easy to make.

1 1/2 cups flour
2 teaspoons baking powder
1/2 teaspoon salt
2 tablespoons sugar
3 tablespoons shortening
1 cup cold cooked rice
1 cup milk
1 egg, beaten

If baking, preheat oven to 425°F. Sift flour, baking powder, salt, and sugar together in bowl. Blend in shortening until mixture is crumbly. Add rice, milk, and egg; mix until dry ingredients are moistened. Batter will be lumpy and rough. Bake 25 minutes, or until golden brown. Serve hot.

Makes 12

Variation

- Steam instead. Cover muffins with lid or tinfoil to keep excess moisture from dripping into pan.

Southern Rice Popovers

Light and tasty.

1/2 cup cold cooked rice
1 cup sifted flour
1 teaspoon baking powder
1 teaspoon grated orange peel
1/2 teaspoon salt
3 teaspoons sugar
1 egg yolk, beaten
2 teaspoons melted butter
1 egg white, beaten until stiff

Preheat oven to 425°F. Heat buttered popover molds. Mix rice with flour, baking powder, orange peel, salt, and sugar. Add egg yolk and melted butter; mix well. Fold in beaten egg white. Fill heated buttered molds half full with batter.

Bake 25 minutes or until tops are firm and golden. Reduce heat to 350°F; bake 10 minutes more. Prick popovers with tines of fork to allow steam to escape. Turn off heat; place on baking sheet. Allow to remain in oven 10 minutes more.

Serves 4 to 6

Philpy

A lovely hot bread from the South. Serve with chicken or pork.

1 cup cooked rice, cooked in milk
$1/2$ cup flour
2 egg yolks
$1/2$ teaspoon salt
2 tablespoons sugar
$1/3$ cup milk
$1/3$ cup sour cream
2 egg whites, beaten until stiff

Stir flour, egg yolks, salt, sugar, and milk into rice. Add sour cream; fold in stiffly beaten egg whites. Put batter in well-greased 9-inch pie plate.

Bake at 375°F for 20 minutes or until golden. Serve hot with butter and honey.

Makes 1 (9-inch) round loaf

Rice Dumplings

Try these chewy dumplings in your favorite stew. Add fresh mint or dill if you wish.

1 1/4 cups cooked rice
2/3 cup flour
2 teaspoons baking powder
3/4 teaspoon salt
1 egg, beaten
1/4 cup milk
1 tablespoon melted butter
Chopped fresh dill or fresh mint (optional)

Mix all ingredients together to make a stiff but light dough. Flavor with mint or dill if you wish. Form into balls; roll in flour and drop into a simmering stew. Cover; cook 15 minutes without lifting the lid.

Serves 4 to 6

Rice Waffles

Light and chewy, these waffles are topped with a honey
and cinnamon sauce.

Waffles

1 3/4 cups flour
4 teaspoons baking powder
1/4 teaspoon salt
2/3 cup cold cooked rice
1 1/3 cups milk
1 egg yolk, beaten
1 tablespoon melted butter
2 egg whites, beaten until stiff

Sauce

1 cup honey
1/2 cup maple syrup
1 teaspoon cinnamon

Sift flour, baking powder, and salt together; mix with rice. Combine milk, egg yolk, and butter; mix with dry ingredients. Fold in egg whites. Cook on lightly greased hot waffle iron. Serve with butter and honey sauce.

To make sauce, combine and heat honey, maple syrup, and cinnamon. Serve over hot waffles.

Serves 4 to 6

Rice Pancakes

Rice adds a nutlike quality.

2 cups flour, sifted
2 teaspoons baking powder
$1/2$ teaspoon salt
2 tablespoons sugar
4 egg yolks, beaten
5 tablespoons shortening
2 cups milk
$1 1/2$ cups cold cooked rice
4 egg whites, beaten until stiff

Sift together dry ingredients in large mixing bowl. Combine egg yolks, shortening, and milk. Stir into dry ingredients; mix well. Add rice to batter; blend well. Fold in beaten egg whites. Stir batter each time before pouring onto hot greased griddle, as rice has a tendency to settle on bottom of mixture.

Serves 4 to 6

Variation

- Add flavorings such as lemon, peanut butter, banana, rum, coconut, or vanilla to batter for a pleasant surprise.

Basic Rice Stuffing

Add your favorite ingredients to rice for an outstanding stuffing.

1 medium onion, minced
1 stalk celery with leaves, chopped
2 tablespoons butter or margarine
1 cup uncooked rice
2 cups chicken broth
Salt and freshly ground black pepper to taste
Pinch of sage and/or thyme (optional)

Sauté onion and celery in butter in nonstick pan until limp. Add rice; sauté until translucent. Combine rice mixture with remaining ingredients in steaming pan. Cover and steam until rice is done, about 20 minutes. Adjust seasoning if necessary. Cool and use as a stuffing.

Makes about 1 quart, enough to stuff a 6- to 8-pound bird

Variations

- *Rice and Mushroom Stuffing:* Sauté 1/2 pound chopped mushrooms with onion and celery.
- *Rice with Raisins and Almonds Stuffing:* Omit celery; substitute 1 1/2 cups beef broth and 1/2 cup sherry for chicken broth. Add 1/2 cup *each* raisins and toasted slivered almonds. Season with nutmeg and allspice.
- *Rice and Chicken Liver Stuffing:* Sauté 1/2 pound chicken livers until browned; remove and mince. Proceed with basic stuffing.
- *Rice and Sausage Stuffing:* Cook sausage until browned. Sauté vegetables in pan. Proceed with basic stuffing.

Basic Wild Rice Stuffing

Wild rice adds elegance to any stuffing. Especially nice with Cornish hens or small game birds.

1 medium onion, minced
1 stalk celery with leaves, minced
2 tablespoons olive oil
1/4 cup minced cooked ham
1 cup wild rice, washed and drained, or 1/2 cup wild rice and
   1/2 cup brown rice, washed and drained
3 cups chicken broth
1/2 teaspoon rosemary or thyme
Salt and freshly ground black pepper to taste

Sauté onion and celery in olive oil until onion is limp and golden. Add ham and rice; sauté until rice is translucent. Combine rice mixture with broth in steaming pan; season with rosemary, salt, and pepper. Cover and steam until rice is done, about 35 minutes. Fluff with fork. Adjust seasoning if necessary.

Makes about 1 quart, enough to stuff a 6- to 8-pound bird

Variation

• Add sausage and/or mushrooms.

Greek Rice Stuffing

This is the stuffing used in the Greek dish *Arni Yemisto*, a crown roast of lamb or a boned leg of lamb filled with rice, livers, currants, and pine nuts.

2 tablespoons olive oil
3/4 cup uncooked rice
1 3/4 cups hot beef broth
2 tablespoons olive oil
1 cup chopped onions
1 clove garlic, minced
1/2 pound chicken livers, diced
1/3 cup currants or raisins
1/2 cup pine nuts or slivered almonds
1/4 cup chopped fresh parsley
2 tablespoons minced fresh mint
Salt and freshly ground black pepper to taste

Sauté rice in olive oil in nonstick pan. Combine rice with broth in steaming pan. Cover and steam until rice is almost done, about 15 minutes.

Meanwhile, sauté onions, garlic, and chicken livers in olive oil in same pan until lightly browned. Mix together cooked rice, sautéed livers, currants, nuts, parsley, mint, salt, and pepper. Adjust seasoning if necessary.

Makes about 1 quart

Variations

- Omit traditional chicken livers from stuffing.
- Stuff lamb fillets with stuffing. Steam until done to taste.

CHAPTER 10

Desserts

After taking the time to prepare such lowfat steamed foods as broccoli or salmon for dinner, it is up to your conscience whether you want to look beyond the recipe for Steamed Apples in this delectable desserts collection. Strawberry Rice Parfait, Apricot-Filled Rice Crepes, Rice Melba, Rice à l'Imperatrice, Polish Rice with Plums, Neapolitan Easter Grain Pie, Dutch Apple Rice, Orange Rice au Grand Marnier and Aunt Rosie's Old-Fashioned Rice Pudding are only a few of the rice desserts you will discover.

Egg custards and puddings, commonly baked, come out smooth and never rubbery when steamed. Steamed puddings, unlike many steamed dishes, are usually cooked partially in water rather than above it. This immersion ensures that these dense mixtures receive the direct, moist heat they need to cook evenly.

Special pans or cups with tightly fitting lids can be ordered with some rice cookers. Otherwise, fashion a lid from tinfoil so that excess moisture won't drip into delicate egg custards. Steaming pan size is another factor to consider when deciding whether to bake or steam a dessert.

Please don't feel restricted by the suggestions that appear with recipes. Use your imagination to create other combinations.

205

Steamed Apples

Fruits retain their natural flavors and texture better when steamed than poached. A touch of cinnamon is added to the apples.

4 medium cooking apples
Cinnamon

Core apples without breaking bottom skin. Sprinkle cinnamon inside each apple. Place in steaming basket; steam 25 to 30 minutes, or until done.

Variations

- Serve with sour cream.
- Steam in steaming pan with red wine.
- Cut apples in quarters. Place in steaming pan. Sprinkle lightly with sugar and a liqueur such as grenadine or brandy.
- Fill with orange marmalade before steaming.

Steamed Pears with Lemon Rice Cream Sauce

An outstanding sauce for any cooked fruit.

1 cup heavy cream, whipped
2 tablespoons sugar
1 tablespoon lemon juice
1/2 teaspoon grated lemon peel
1/4 teaspoon vanilla
Dash of nutmeg
1 cup cold cooked rice
4 chilled whole steamed pears

Whip cream. Add sugar, lemon juice and peel, vanilla, and nutmeg. Fold into cold cooked rice. Chill. Top individual steamed pears with cream sauce before serving.

Serves 4

Basic Dessert Rice

This basic sweet rice can be used as a base for countless desserts. Just vary the flavorings; add nuts, fresh fruits, and dried and candied fruits and citron. Short or medium grain rices are recommended for desserts.

3 cups hot milk
1 cup uncooked rice
Pinch of salt
5 tablespoons sugar
1 cup heavy cream
2 tablespoons butter

Combine milk with rice, salt, and sugar in steaming pan. Cover and steam until rice is tender and creamy, 20 to 25 minutes. When cooked, add cream and butter. Add more sugar if desired.

Variations

- *Rice Flan or Tart*: Fill dessert pie shell with dessert rice not quite to the top. Sprinkle with sugar. Bake at 350°F for 25 to 30 minutes until golden. Serve hot or cold. Chopped crystallized fruit soaked in kirsch or other liqueur is a happy addition.
- *Rice Flan or Tart with Fruit*: Proceed as in previous recipe, but fill pie shell only three-quarters full. Place raw apricots soaked in kirsch and sugar on top of rice. Sprinkle with sugar. Spread top of flan with strained apricot jam diluted with a little syrup.
- In the same way, flans can be made with other fruits such as: bananas (cut in rounds or sliced lengthwise), cherries, pears (in quarters and half-cooked in syrup), peaches, apples, and plums.
- *Rice with Caramel*: Fill large charlotte mold lined with caramelized sugar with dessert rice. Bake in oven in pan of water for 25 to 30 minutes. Unmold. Serve hot or cold.
- *Rice with Fruit*: Layer dessert rice flavored with vanilla in glass bowl, alternating with slices of fruit and a colorful fruit such as raspberries in syrup.

Almond Rice Pudding

Swedish families serve this dessert at Christmas.

1 cup uncooked rice
½ cup sugar
Pinch of salt
3½ cups milk
¼ cup cream sherry
1 tablespoon vanilla
1 cup toasted slivered almonds
2 cups heavy cream

Combine rice, sugar, salt, and milk in steaming pan. Cover and steam until rice is creamy, 20 to 25 minutes. Stir once during cooking time. Cool slightly.

Stir in sherry, vanilla, and almonds. Whip cream until soft peaks form. Fold into rice mixture. Cover and chill overnight. Serve with lingonberry preserves for a special treat.

Serves 4 to 6

Variation

- Bury a whole almond in the center. Whoever gets the almond, some say, will marry within the year.

Dutch Apple Rice

A yummy favorite filled with raisins and apple.

2 cups cooked rice
1/2 cup milk
1/3 cup raisins
1 egg, beaten
1/3 cup sugar
1/2 teaspoon salt
1/4 teaspoon cinnamon
1 tablespoon butter
2 cups steamed, peeled apple slices
Dash of nutmeg

Combine cooked rice, milk, raisins, egg, sugar, salt, cinnamon, and butter in pan. Simmer, stirring occasionally, until blended. Stir in apple slices. Pour into serving dishes; chill. Sprinkle with nutmeg before serving.

Serves 4 to 6

Orange Rice au Grand Marnier

Flavoring orange rice pudding with Grand Marnier makes it a dish fit for royalty.

³/₄ cup uncooked rice
3 cups milk
Pinch of salt
1 ¹/₂ teaspoons grated orange peel
¹/₂ cup orange juice
³/₄ cup heavy cream, whipped
2 cups orange sections
¹/₃ cup Grand Marnier

Combine rice with milk and salt in steaming pan. Cover and steam until rice is done, about 20 minutes. Cool slightly.

Mix cooked rice with orange peel, orange juice, and whipped cream. Layer rice mixture with orange sections; top with Grand Marnier. Chill if desired.

Serves 4 to 6

Pineapple Rice Pudding

Whipped cream and pineapple is folded into chilled creamy rice before serving.

1/2 cup uncooked rice
2 cups milk
1/4 cup sugar
Pinch of salt
1/2 teaspoon vanilla
1/4 teaspoon nutmeg
1/4 cup milk
1/2 cup heavy cream, whipped
1/2 cup crushed pineapple, drained

Combine rice with milk, sugar, and salt in steaming pan. Cover and steam until rice is done, about 20 minutes. Cool slightly.

Stir in vanilla, nutmeg, and milk. Refrigerate until well chilled. Fold in whipped cream and pineapple before serving.

Serves 4

Polish Rice with Plums

Other fruits such as sliced peaches can be used.

2 cups cooked rice
2 cups canned pitted plums, undrained
1 tablespoon sugar
1/2 teaspoon cinnamon
1 cup sour cream
3 tablespoons sugar

Arrange cooked rice and plums in layers, beginning with rice first. Sprinkle with cinnamon and sugar. Continue until all ingredients are used up. Refrigerate 2 hours. Beat sour cream with sugar. Serve over chilled rice.

Serves 4

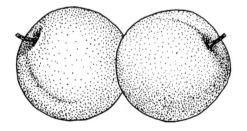

Rice Romanoff

Flavored with liqueur and filled with toasted almonds, this dessert is a great ending for any important dinner.

3 cups heavy cream
3 tablespoons kirsch, Grand Marnier, or cognac
3 tablespoons sugar
1/2 cup blanched slivered almonds
3 cups cooked rice
20 macaroons, soaked in kirsch, Grand Marnier, or cognac

Whip cream until stiff; flavor with liquor and sugar. Stir in almonds. Blend whipped cream mixture thoroughly with cooked rice. Place one-third of rice cream in glass serving bowl. Arrange half of the macaroons on top. Add another one-third of rice cream, then the remaining macaroons. Finish with rice cream. Chill. Serve with raspberry sauce.

Serves 4 to 6

Strawberry Rice Parfait

Strawberries and whipped cream make this one of the prettiest and tastiest desserts you can serve.

1 cup uncooked rice
2¹/₂ tablespoons sugar
2 cups cold water
¹/₂ pint heavy cream
2 tablespoons sugar
¹/₂ teaspoon almond extract
1 (10-ounce) package frozen strawberries, thawed

Combine rice, sugar, and water in steaming pan. Cover and steam until rice is done, about 20 minutes. Chill.

Just before serving, whip heavy cream; blend in sugar and almond flavoring. Reserve enough whipped cream for garnish, then fold into chilled rice. Fill parfait glasses with alternate layers of rice mixture and strawberries, ending with the reserved whipped cream. Put strawberry on top.

Serves 4

Old-Fashioned Rice Pudding

A superb baked rice pudding filled with plump raisins which my ninety-three-year-old aunt Rosie makes better than anyone.

3 cups milk
3 large eggs, beaten
$1/2$ cup sugar
$1/2$ teaspoon salt
1 cup cooked rice
1 teaspoon vanilla
$1/2$ cup raisins

Scald or heat milk in saucepan until almost boiling; allow hot milk to cool slightly. Mix together eggs, sugar, and salt in $1 1/2$-quart baking dish. Add hot milk slowly, stirring constantly.

Stir in cooked rice, vanilla, and raisins. Place baking dish in pan containing an inch of hot water in oven. Bake at 350°F for 1 hour or until golden. Stir once after pudding has been in oven 15 minutes.

Serves 6

Variation

• Steam pudding instead. Cover pudding with lid or tinfoil to keep excess moisture from dripping into pan.

Baked Apricot Pudding

Apricot jam makes this pudding both pretty and delicious.

1 cup cooked rice
1/4 cup sugar
Pinch of salt
2 eggs, beaten
2/3 cup milk
2/3 cup light cream
1 tablespoon grated lemon peel
3 tablespoons apricot jam
1/3 cup chopped almonds or pecans
Sour cream

Combine cooked rice with sugar and salt. Beat eggs until very thick and lemon colored; fold into rice mixture. Mix with milk, cream, lemon peel, and 1 tablespoon apricot jam. Pour into buttered baking dish. Spread with rest of apricot jam; sprinkle with almonds.

Bake in 350°F oven for 20 to 30 minutes or until pudding is firm and golden. Serve warm with sour cream.

Serves 4

Rice Pudding with Candied Fruit

A spectacular dessert garnished with whipped cream
and raspberry jam.

3 cups hot milk
3 cups cooked rice
3/4 cup sugar
2 tablespoons butter
4 eggs, beaten
2 teaspoons vanilla
3/4 cup candied fruit, soaked in 2 1/2 tablespoons rum
Pinch of salt
1/4 cup sugar
2 tablespoons water
Whipped cream or melted raspberry jam

Combine hot milk and cooked rice in steaming pan. Cover and
steam 15 minutes. Cool slightly. Add sugar, butter, and eggs;
blend well. Add vanilla, candied fruit, and salt; blend well. Melt
remaining sugar with water in charlotte mold or other straight-
sided baking dish. When sugar is light brown, tilt mold so syrup
will cover the bottom and sides. Fill with rice mixture; place in
pan of hot water.

Bake for 30 minutes at 350°F. Cool to lukewarm. Unmold.
Garnish with whipped cream or melted raspberry jam.

Serves 6 to 8

Variation

• Steam instead. Cover pudding with lid or tinfoil to keep excess moisture from dripping into pan.

Orange Rice Custard

An orange-flavored rice custard. Serve with chicken or duck, or top with honey for dessert.

1 cup uncooked rice
2 1/2 cups hot milk
Pinch of salt
3 eggs, beaten
1 tablespoon butter, at room temperature
Juice of 1 orange
2 tablespoons grated orange peel
1 tablespoon sesame seeds

Combine rice with milk and salt in steaming pan. Cover and steam until rice is done, about 20 minutes. Mix rice with eggs, butter, orange juice, orange peel, and sesame seeds. Fill baking pan with rice mixture; place in pan of hot water. Bake 30 minutes at 300°F, until custard is firm and golden.

Serves 6

Variation

• Steam instead. Cover pudding with lid or tinfoil to keep excess moisture from dripping into pan.

Baked Peach and Rice Custard

Peaches and rice are layered in this marvelously tasty custard dessert.

2 1/2 cups milk
2 eggs, beaten
1/4 cup sugar
1/2 teaspoon salt
2 cups cooked rice
1/2 teaspoon almond extract
2 cups canned peaches, drained
2 tablespoons brown sugar
Cream

To make custard, combine milk, eggs, sugar, and salt in top of double boiler; cook over boiling water, stirring constantly, 20 minutes or until thickened. Remove from heat.

Stir in rice and almond extract. In buttered casserole, alternate layers of peaches and rice, beginning with rice and ending with peaches. Sprinkle top with brown sugar. Bake 30 minutes at 350°F or until custard is set. Serve warm or cold with cream.

Serves 4

Rice Melba

As beautiful and tasty as the original melba made with ice cream.

2/3 cup uncooked rice
2 cups milk
1/3 cup sugar
1/4 teaspoon salt
Pinch of nutmeg
Pinch of cinnamon
1 cup heavy cream
6 canned peach halves, drained
1/2 cup red currant or raspberry jelly

Combine rice and milk in steaming pan. Cover and steam until rice is done, about 20 minutes. Stir in sugar, salt, nutmeg, and cinnamon. Cool.

Whip cream. Fold chilled rice into cream. Spoon into dessert dishes. Put peach half on top, cut side down. Heat jelly; pour a little over each peach.

Serves 6

Rice à l'Imperatrice

Candied fruit, kirsch, walnuts, and whipped cream combine to make this creamy dessert both extraordinarily good and impressively decorative for your most important dinners. But it is time consuming.

3/4 cup mixed candied fruits, finely chopped
1/3 cup kirsch
1/2 cup walnuts, chopped
1/4 cup kirsch
1/2 cup uncooked rice
1 3/4 cups milk
4 egg yolks, beaten
1/2 cup sugar
3/4 cup milk
1/2 teaspoon vanilla extract
1 envelope unflavored gelatin
2 tablespoons cold water
1 cup heavy cream, whipped
2/3 cup currant jelly

Marinate fruits in kirsch. Reserve.
    Marinate nuts in kirsch. Reserve.
    Combine rice and milk in steaming pan. Cover and steam until rice is done, about 20 minutes.
    Meanwhile, combine egg yolks with sugar, milk, and vanilla in top of double boiler. Cook over boiling water, stirring constantly, until thickened. Soften gelatin in cold water; stir into milk-egg mixture. Add cooked rice; blend well. Chill until mixture begins to set.
    Fold in 1/2 cup marinated fruit and whipped cream. Spoon rice mixture into 8-inch ring mold. Chill at least 4 hours; unmold. Mix marinated nuts into jelly; sprinkle on top and around mold. Decorate with remaining fruit.

Serves 6

Rice and Ricotta Cheese Bake

Warmed jam tops this easy-to-prepare baked rice dessert made with ricotta cheese.

2 egg yolks, beaten
3 tablespoons sugar
1 1/4 cups ricotta cheese
2 cups cooked rice
2 egg whites, beaten stiff
1/2 cup cake crumbs
1 cup raspberry, peach, or currant jam, warmed

Preheat oven to 400°F. Beat egg yolks with sugar; combine with cheese until well blended. Add cooked rice; mix well. Fold in egg whites; pour into buttered tube pan which has been sprinkled with cake crumbs.

Bake in oven 30 minutes. Remove from pan. Serve hot or cold with warmed jam poured over top.

Serves 4

Apricot Rice Soufflé

Soufflés have an undeserved reputation for being difficult to make. This delicious dessert will prove otherwise.

¹/₄ cup butter
¹/₄ cup flour
1 cup milk
Pinch of salt
4 egg yolks, slightly beaten
1 cup cooked rice
1 cup apricot pulp
¹/₃ cup sugar
1 tablespoon apricot brandy or to taste
4 egg whites, beaten until stiff but not dry

Preheat oven to 325°F. In saucepan, stir flour into melted butter to make a roux. Blend in milk and salt. Cook, stirring constantly, until thickened. Remove from heat. Cool slightly.

Combine white sauce with beaten egg yolks and cooked rice. Add apricot pulp, sugar, and apricot brandy to rice mixture; mix thoroughly. Fold in beaten egg whites. Pour into ungreased 2-quart soufflé dish. Bake 1 hour in oven. Serve immediately.

Serves 4

Rice Cake

A cake filled with candied citron and almonds.

6 1/2 cups milk
1 1/2 cups rice
Pinch of salt
1 cup sugar
4 egg yolks
Grated peel of 1 lemon or orange
1/2 cup diced candied citron
1 teaspoon vanilla
1/2 cup toasted chopped almonds
4 egg whites, at room temperature
Fine dry cake or bread crumbs
1/4 cup Maraschino
Powdered sugar

Combine milk, rice, salt, and 1/2 cup sugar in steaming pan. Cover and steam until rice is done, about 20 minutes. Allow to cool.

Beat egg yolks with remaining 1/2 cup sugar until blended. Stir in rice mixture, grated peel, candied citron, vanilla, and almonds. Beat egg whites until stiff; fold into mixture.

Butter well a 12-inch cake pan; coat with cake or bread crumbs. Pour rice mixture into pan. Bake at 325°F for 1 1/2 hours. The cake should be firm with a golden brown top. Cool. Prick when cool with a toothpick; sprinkle with Maraschino. Allow to lay overnight. Dust with powdered sugar before serving.

Makes 1 (12-inch) cake

Neapolitan Easter Grain Pie

The original uses whole wheat softened for 3 days and cooked in milk. This version using rice is just as delicious.

2 1/2 cups milk
2/3 cup uncooked rice
Pinch of salt

Filling

1 pound ricotta
1 1/2 cups sugar
4 eggs
1/2 cup citron
Grated peel of 1 orange
1 teaspoon vanilla
1 (10-inch) unbaked pie shell plus dough for lattice top

Combine milk, rice, and salt in steaming pan. Cover and steam until rice is done, about 20 minutes. Cool.

Beat ricotta and sugar together until smooth. Add eggs one at a time, beating well after each addition. Add citron, orange peel, and vanilla; blend well. Fold in cooked rice. Pour mixture into unbaked pie shell; top with lattice strips. Flute edges.

Bake in 425°F oven for 15 minutes. Lower heat to 350°F; continue baking for 45 minutes, or until firm in the center and golden.

Makes 1 (10-inch) pie

Variations

• Add grated chocolate.
• Make as tarts instead.

Kolwadjik

Cape Malays contributed this rice cake to the South African dessert repertoire.

3 1/2 cups hot cooked rice
1/2 cup sugar
1 teaspoon cinnamon
1/4 teaspoon cardamom
1/4 cup butter
2 cups shredded coconut

Combine hot cooked rice with sugar, cinnamon, cardamon, butter, and coconut. Press into 9- by 13- by 2-inch baking pan; cool. Cut into diamonds; serve like cake.

Makes 1 (9 by 13-inch) cake

Apricot-Filled Rice Crepes

Canned pie filling makes this an easy dessert.

Crepes
1/2 cup flour
1/4 teaspoon salt
1 tablespoon sugar
2 eggs, beaten
1/2 cup milk
1 tablespoon cold water
1 tablespoon melted butter or margarine
1/2 cup cooked rice

Filling
1 can apricot pie filling
Powdered sugar

Sift flour, salt, and sugar together in bowl. Mix together eggs, milk, water, and butter. Add slowly to dry ingredients, beating until smooth. Mix in cooked rice. Allow to rest 10 minutes.

To make crepes, brush bottom and sides of 6-inch crepe pan or skillet with cooking oil; set over moderate heat. Stir batter; add 2 tablespoons to skillet, tipping it back and forth so batter just coats bottom. Brown lightly on one side; turn and brown the other side. Keep warm in 250°F oven until all crepes are made. Cook remaining crepes the same way.

Heat pie filling. To serve, spread crepe with pie filling; roll up and sprinkle with powdered sugar.

Makes 10 crepes

INDEX